Youth and Change
in American Politics

Youth and Change in American Politics

Louis M. Seagull

New Viewpoints
A Division of Franklin Watts
New York / London / 1977

Library of Congress Cataloging in Publication Data

Seagull, Louis M
  Youth & change in American politics.

  Bibliography: p.
  Includes index.
  1. Youth—United States—Political activity.
2. Elections—United States.   I. Title.
HQ796.S42   301.5'92   77–4315
ISBN 0–531–05395–4
ISBN 0–531–05605–8 pbk.

New Viewpoints
A Division of Franklin Watts
730 Fifth Avenue
New York, New York 10019

To Fanya and Amon

Preface

This book is an attempt to use the phenomenon of the youth vote as a device for gauging the dynamics of present and future American politics. Accordingly, the scope of this study is not confined to any special or exclusive concern with the outcome of elections in the early 1970s when, in fact, the youth vote was a topic of fleeting interest. Instead, the quest is for those underlying dynamics which may render comprehensible the outcomes and, more importantly, the sociological patterns in any number of elections.

The following essays, all written for this book, represent a genre of social science research and writing which combines elements of behavioral analysis and personal opinion. Essentially, the form is that of the essay. The opportunity to do this book was a chance to put to service my long-standing interest in political sociology as well as to express my belief that the study of political behavior should be conducted within a political context, which in this case is present American politics.

My basic assumption is that there is integrity and legitimacy in and for the study of American politics. Accordingly, the elements which constitute American political behavior are not used as a "data base" to test some theoretical notions. Instead, behavioral theories are selected and employed when they can contribute to an understanding of American politics. The challenge facing students of American politics is to pick interesting subjects to study, and then to bring to bear the theories and methods of political behavior, as well as other intellectual constructs, to illuminate them.

I owe my involvement with this project to Henry J. Abraham, now of the University of Virginia, who originally steered to me a request to do an article on the youth vote. Gerald Pomper, at Rutgers University, and Andrew Baggaley, of the Graduate School of Education, University of Pennsylvania, provided helpful commentaries on an earlier draft, some of which I have accepted. And, as before, a special debt of gratitude is expressed to my wife, Rhea, for her encouragement and efforts to help simplify and clarify my language. The dedication is to our children, in the hope that this book may still be found interesting when they are old enough to read and understand it.

L.M.S.

Contents

Youth and Change
in American Politics

1 | Youth and American Politics

For most of the post-World War II years the lowering of the voting age had been a minor item on the agenda of the U.S. Congress from time to time. Finally, in 1970, Congress added an amendment to its major civil rights bill of that Congress, the Voting Rights Act of 1970, a provision enfranchising citizens aged eighteen to twenty-one. According to this legislation the age for suffrage was to be lowered on January 1, 1971, for state and local as well as federal elections. However, on December 21, 1970, the Supreme Court ruled that Congress itself could lower the voting age for federal elections only, not for state and local ones.

The administrative and financial problems of maintaining two sets of registration books, ballots, and voting machines was potentially immense. Because of this potential burden, Congress initiated again the lowering of the suffrage, but this time as an amendment to the U.S. Constitution. On March 23, 1971, Congress sent the proposed amendment to the Constitution to the states. Approval of the Twenty-sixth Amendment by the requisite thirty-eight states came in record time, by June 30, 1971.

This expansion of the suffrage precipitated the inquiry of this book. But the subject of the book was due for consideration in any event and irrespective of the Twenty-sixth Amendment. More generally, appraisals of American society and politics in the last third of the twentieth century will have to confront two bizarre and unprecedented phenomena—the emergence of youth as a special force in the marketplace and as social critic, and the changed character of the political institutions. Political parties and institutions have fallen into disrepute and disuse. And although a spirit of reform and revitalization is afoot, its expression inspires only a small minority. Yet, this minority has the potential to transform the character of American politics. Whether this is good or bad is not the province of this essay. Instead, the aim of this study is to contribute toward an explanation of the politically relevant behavior of youth and in turn the impact of youth on party and political systems.

The examination of youth is confounded by the very heterogeneity of the subject. The age group eighteen to twenty-four contains segments in college, in the armed forces, in the labor force, among the unemployed, and housepersons. Much of this analysis will deal with the college-educated because education is the special attribute of this age group in the aggregate. But the general attributes and implications of modern society provide a framework for understanding all youth, not just those in college. Accordingly, the study employs a macro or societal perspective in the attempt to confront both the apathy and unconcern of most youth and the extraordinary concern and involvement of a minority of them.

To deal with societal tendencies on one hand and political ones on the other is to invoke the perspectives of political sociology. These perspectives do not suggest that everything political is consequent to things social; that would be nothing more than simplistic social determinism. Yet, developments in society and polity do have implications for one another. This study seeks to attend to these implications. It aims to use the youth phenomenon in order to interpret recent tendencies in American politics. And while the specific focus is on the expansion of the electorate to youth and the consequences of this expansion, the larger concern is with youth more generally and its meaning in American society and politics.

Any analysis of youth must consider whether those aged eighteen to twenty-four behave differently than those in other age categories. Yet, the possible impact and full meaning of the youth vote can not be illuminated in any single election. Rather, the potential contributions of youth in politics must be inferred from social science theory and research, as well as from the comparisons of the empirical record of the political behavior of young persons with older ones. This empirical record is broader than just voting statistics. It includes participation in party organizations and political involvement in movements. It also includes public opinion, which increasingly is a basis for political action and nonaction. This essay assumes that the youth vote does and will matter. It is the task of analysis to delineate the different dimensions of this impact and to relate them to the pattern of cleavages and partisan change.

The analysis must also confront the disjuncture between the expectation and reality of youth's behavior and delineate the

role of youth in American politics. Thus, this study is both
essay and hypothesis. It employs some of the concepts of political sociology to interpret American politics and postulates
the impact and meaning of youth for this politics.

The analysis of the youth vote compels a two-sided inquiry. On one hand there is the need to explain the political
behavior of youth; on the other hand it is important to probe
the consequences of youth for American politics. In the first
instance youth is a dependent phenomenon whose political
patterns are a response to societal factors. In the second instance these patterns serve as the independent variables which
impact upon the evolving political system. The importance of
the double-edged inquiry lies in its illumination of otherwise
disparate and ad hoc facts of political behavior. The study of
political behavior thereby assumes its proper place in political analysis.

The Distinctiveness of Youth

Even in the absence of the Twenty-sixth Amendment to
the U.S. Constitution, which enfranchised those eighteen to
twenty years of age, it would have been appropriate to study
youth's political involvement. For whether the age of political
majority is eighteen or twenty-one is less important than the
population bulge which altered the demographic shape of
American society in the 1960s. As Samuel Lubell has
noted, ". . . the 1964 count of eighteen-year-old males stood at
roughly 1,401,000. Just one year later the figure had jumped
35 per cent, to 1,897,000, continuing at roughly that level
in the years after." [1] This youth bulge in the population reflected the baby boom of some two decades previous. This is

1. Samuel Lubell, *The Hidden Crisis in American Politics* (New York:
W. W. Norton, 1971), pp. 182–83.

the same generation which crowded the colleges in the middle and late 1960s, sustained the student protests in these institutions, and some of whose members were active in 1968 Democratic presidential nomination politics. Thus, it would not be difficult to justify interest in this phenomenon even had there not been the Twenty-sixth Amendment.

The population bulge provided the necessary ingredient —numbers—for making a case for the potentially distinctive character of youth in recent years. However, other factors— the ubiquity of the mass media, relative affluence, and, most importantly, the education revolution—provided the sufficient ingredients to render this potential into reality.

A major factor setting this generation apart from previous ones is its exposure to television—particularly at the time when the television industry's investment and proficiency in news reporting accelerated greatly. Both mass education and exposure to television contributed to a lessening of parental influence in the political socialization process. This change in technology is important in any account of the possible gap between the political orientations of the newly enfranchised generation and their parents. And, together with the effects of relative affluence, the mass media contributed to the emergence of a youth market.

Affluence is the second major characteristic that touched a large portion of those who came of age politically in the 1970s and late 1960s. The effects of affluence itself are difficult to probe, partly because the concept is very diffuse and partly because of its correlation with other variables whose meanings were better established, such as education. For some, affluence meant freedom from the constraint of earning life's necessities. In a society in which a multitude of consumer goods and amenities are easily available, the dependent status of many of the elite college students was a comfortable one. The idealism and social commitment which many of them exhibited in the late 1960s was a function, in part, of their freedom and comfort, together with their learning of the discrepancy between the ideal and the real in social and political relations.

The source of the affluence that peaked in the late 1960s is noteworthy also. Increasingly, the living standards of the middle class resulted less from the effort and enterprise of the competitive individual postulated by classical economic liberalism. Instead, it was through the benefits of life and work in the large-scale collective and bureaucratic enterprise—the corporation, the university, the labor union, and the foundation— that many Americans seemed to have achieved the good life.

Government employment and government contracts themselves were important props for the new middle class. These new sources of affluence reflected a structural change in the character of the economic order which served to indict classical liberal social and economic theory. For some, affluence was a liberating condition which opened up the possibility of avoiding economic production and instead indulging in social and political criticism. For others, the very notion of individual hard work and competition was replaced by that of cooperation and community. In this sense as well, affluence had a liberating effect.

It is obvious that these perspectives of the 1960s seem very remote from the economic reality of the mid-1970s. Indeed, much of the affluence has been negated by inflation and withdrawn by the constricted budgets of governments, universities, foundations, and firms. Neither the public nor the private sectors seem capable of supporting the standards of living which so many had taken for granted, especially among the middle class.

Of all changes in the American electorate over time, the rising levels of education of the electorate are the most momentous. Education is the hallmark of modern societies and is important to these societies in two principal respects. First, mass education sustains the advanced technological civilizations by providing the manpower with the requisite basic and advanced skills. Secondly, mass higher education makes possible the ethos of egalitarianism and of status by achievement and merit rather than ascription. Both purposes were pursued by America in the 1960s in response to the recognition of Soviet technological advances, as exemplified by the launching of Sputnik in 1958. Not coincidentally, the vehicle for many of the educational opportunities of the recent past were the National Defense Education acts.

It is mass higher education especially that sets the new generation apart from previous new ones. Even given the fact that less than a majority (roughly about 40 per cent) of young people have experienced higher education recently, this still presents a novel social condition. Never before, or even elsewhere today, has such a considerable segment of young people been touched in this manner. For those resident in college or university, higher education means increased exposure to peer groups and segregation from other age groups or social situations. In this respect education contributes to the institutionalization of age-based roles and types.

It is ironic that it was the federal budget which fueled the education revolution in the 1960s and it is the federal budget which is leading to unemployment for so many of the young educated in the 1970s.[2] A decade ago many educated youth felt a sense of betrayal out of the discrepancy between the American values inculcated and the reality perceived. This was

2. Richard Flacks, *Youth and Social Change* (Chicago: Markham, 1971), p. 106.

one condition, among others to be sure, for the student movement. There is a similar sense of betrayal today between the promise of education and the reality of economic opportunity. Such discrepancies contribute to a series of conflicts in modern life.

The View from '72

Prior to the 1972 presidential election, political practitioners and many journalists viewed with varying degrees of optimism, apprehension, and eager curiosity the possible behavior and impact of approximately 11 million persons of a previously untried electoral category. This eighteen to twenty-one segment included 4 million college students, 4.1 million full-time workers, 1 million housewives, 900,000 high school students, and 800,000 armed forces personnel.[3] Total potential new voters numbered approximately 25 million, including those over twenty-one who had been too young to vote in the previous presidential election. Apprehensions and expectations were heightened following the very close 1968 presidential election and the memory of the very close one in 1960. In state after state, the number of possible new young voters exceeded the victory margins of 1968.

In retrospect, the comparison with 1968 was an unfortunate one inasmuch as the close margin of Richard M. Nixon over Hubert H. Humphrey owned much to the presence of George C. Wallace on the ballot, which split the protest and opposition vote. Much of Wallace's 1968 vote would likely have been Nixon's in that year had Wallace not been on the ballot. At the same time, most academic analysts of voting behavior discounted the youth vote, expecting youth to ex-

3. U.S. Census figures summarized in Sidney Hyman, *Youth in Politics: Expectations and Realities* (New York: Basic Books, 1972), p. 6.

hibit the lowest rate of voting participation for any age category as well as simply replicating parental tendencies. And in the aftermath of Nixon's 1972 landslide, interest in the youth vote evaporated even faster than it had materialized.

This recent unconcern with the youth vote was an unfortunate development which could happen only when the wrong facts were considered. For while victory or defeat are the concerns often ascribed to most politicians, they are really not that important to the political scientist. In the case of 1972 it was surely unreal to expect that youth could elect a candidate, George McGovern, when so much else seemed to conspire against him. Similarly, it would be folly to dismiss the possible impact of the youth vote and, more importantly, the character, direction, and meaning of youthful participation in politics in the years after 1972. It would be unfortunate even to ignore youth's patterns in the 1972 balloting, for they reveal much. In that year voters eighteen to twenty-four years of age were disproportionately Democratic in comparison with older voters. Approximately half of the young voters chose McGovern as compared to a bit more than a third of the middle-aged voters, as Table 1 reveals. Obviously, this record falls short of any expectation that the youth vote would be massively Democratic, but it does reflect a Democratic proclivity even in a very bad Democratic presidential year. Quite simply, youth were considerably more Democratic than any other age group. Comparisons such as these are precisely the ones the political analysts ought to make in order to be able to place in perspective Nixon's election-night claim of gathering a majority even among first-voting young Americans. In comparison with the politics of other groups, such a claim assumes a hollow ring.

Table 1 | Age by Vote: 1972

Age	McGovern	Nixon	Base N.	Tot. %
18–24	50.5%	49.5%	202	100.0%
25–34	39.5	60.5	334	100.0
35–54	33.7	66.3	570	100.0
55+	29.2	70.8	473	100.0

Gamma = .21

Gamma is a coefficient used to reflect the association between two ordinal or ranked response variables. Essentially, it is a measure relating position on one variable with position on a second variable. There need not be any absolute basis to a high or low ranking of values on a variable. The researcher can assign polarities, high, low, and positions in between, on bases suitable to the research needs. In this instance, Gamma of .21 indicates a modest positive association between being younger and voting for McGovern.

SOURCE: The election studies of the Center for Political Studies, provided through the Inter-University Consortium for Political Research.

The record of young voters in 1972 takes on importance from another perspective as well. The national electoral response in that year was a massive dislocation of the vote, at least on the presidential level, as Nixon captured the overwhelming support of older white voters. The national political expression in that year resembled less the character of routine party politics than it did that of a movement dominated by concern for one unique issue package—the personality of McGovern and the constituency and concerns which he was perceived to represent. Given the movement character of 1972 Republican political patterns, it would be surprising if youth, who are less firmly attached to existing political parties and patterns, were not affected by the tug toward Nixon. Yet, half of the voting young still voted Democratic, despite the fact that their dominant party identification is independent. And for those young voters who were Democratic identifiers, loyalty to their party's nominee exceeded that for any other Democratic age group.[4] These perspectives suggest that, in a more usual Democratic year, the Democratic proclivity of young voters could be even more pronounced.

Youth and New Routines
in American Politics

This study aims to explain the behavior of youth and to illuminate three emerging tendencies in American politics—the recent secular, or long-term, decline in voting participation, the altered style of political action, and the changing content and cleavage of public opinion. These tendencies are interrelated. Moreover, youth impacts disproportionately on each of these tendencies. Thus, the major effect of youth in politics is not the replication of the status quo but rather the acceleration of political change.

Voting turnout has been on a continuing decline since 1960. If the traditionally lower voting participation rates of young persons in the aggregate continue, this could continue to depress the overall turnout in the population. The reasons for nonparticipation are manifold and complex. Two basic ones, however, stand out and lead to two very different interpretations of the state of the political process at this time. Simple lack of interest is a long-standing reason for nonparticipation and is associated with lower education levels and a lower sense of political efficacy. Overabundant interest, coupled with issue commitments and orientations not represented by the structure of party conflict, is a second source of declining participation.

4. Gerald M. Pomper, *Voters' Choice* (New York: Dodd, Mead, 1975), pp. 92–93.

For if simple lack of interest were responsibile for non-participation, there would at least be the expectation that higher rates of educational achievement could go far to alleviate the problem. But the second reason for nonparticipation reflects a fundamental incompatibility between the evolution of society and established political institutions, particularly the party institutions. Theodore J. Lowi has written that abstention is a rational strategy when issues are not presented or are irrelevant to the concerns of the people.[5] According to Lowi, nonvoting can be viewed as a "third party," which, true to the character of third-party movements, would raise the lack of choice and articulation as an issue.

A third reason for nonparticipation is also possible. If citizens feel that voting is futile, that neither of the major parties or candidates would make any difference for the country or their lives, there is no compulsion to vote, except out of habit or civic duty. Thus, lack of interest, the non-representativeness of the contending candidates, and a possible disillusionment with politics generally are all plausible reasons for the decline in voting participation.

The impact of youth on participation rates is not without ambiguity. In the aggregate the youth population demonstrates greater variability in participation than any other age category. The college-educated young participate at a very high rate; the uneducated young participate at a very low rate. In any event it would be erroneous to blame lower voting turnout on the suffrage expansion. Quite simply, the decline in voting participation began in earnest prior to the expansion of the electorate, and is surely related to other causes. What is important, however, is that the direction of highly motivated youth's participation has been away from centrist and consensus candidates.

5. Theodore J. Lowi, *The Nation*, December 18, 1972.

The direction of youth's participation repudiates, therefore, a major theme of American political history, which emphasizes the politics of coalition and central position. As Andrew M. Greeley summarizes this tradition, American political history has been based upon divergent viewpoints and interests, but ones inherently coalitional.[6] Furthermore, societal consensus has long been a presumed condition for the American two-party system, while in turn political consensus has been one of the consequences of this political process. These orthodox perspectives have been challenged in recent years by the rise of noncentrist candidates for the presidency, such as Republican Senator Barry Goldwater in 1964, Governor George Wallace in 1968, Democratic Senator Eugene McCarthy in 1968, and Democratic Senator George McGovern in 1972. Age-related political polarization can only contribute to this tendency. Compared to older voters, younger ones disproportionately supported first McCarthy and later Wallace in 1968 and McGovern in 1972.

Few aspects of democratic government are as important as the structuring of choice. For therein lies the currency of politics at any given time. Thus, youth's disproportionate support of the noncentrist candidates and appeals—be it for the person of George Wallace, Eugene McCarthy, or George McGovern—warrants our most serious attention. The defeat of these candidates is not as important as the appeals they were able to champion or the political opportunities they yielded to their centrist oppositions. The year 1972 is a case in point. To structure choice is to structure American politics. And it is this potential that is so important about youth and its contributions to American politics.

6. Andrew M. Greeley, *Building Coalitions: American Politics in the 1970s* (New York: New Viewpoints, A Division of Franklin Watts, 1974).

The choices before the electorate reveal something of the character of the underlying political alignments and these alignments' hold upon the electorate. Indeed, of all things changing in American politics, none are more important than the character of the political alignments and the choices which they permit to be offered to the electorate. The historic succession of alignment era upon alignment era may no longer hold in a period characterized by extreme electoral instability together with widespread malaise and cynicism. This very instability, malaise, and, on the part of some young persons, lack of attachment to conventional parties and partisans, represents a possible opportunity for the emergence of a new political order. Past electoral cleavages are less and less the basis for political division and political commitment.

American political cleavages and institutions are in a state of unresolved flux in response to the changing patterns of socialization and social structure. The impact of the mass media of communication, particularly television, and mass higher education represent a challenge to the traditional models of socialization, which emphasized early political learning and intergenerational continuity. Moreover, region and class no longer predict partisanship in the manner they once did, especially for the young.

In considerable measure, therefore, mass social and governmental relations, together with the attitudes associated with life and work in a post-industrial society, are changing the individual's political orientations. New value climates and new styles of political participation challenge the dominance of party as an institution in our society and elevate the importance of social movements as alternative mechanisms of democratic government. Political protests, especially by youth, received an early impetus in the southern civil rights crusades of the early 1960s. They were reinforced by the confrontations with the universities, beginning with the Free Speech Movement at the University of California-Berkeley in 1964. And they continued in the antiwar movement, in the 1968 presidential campaigns of Eugene McCarthy and Robert Kennedy, and the 1968 protests at Columbia University. Throughout this period, positions that initially seemed extreme and the province of a minority of young people gained in time a wider acceptance and near conventionality. It is in this sense that the young are in the vanguard of change and one reason why it is important to study the youth segment of the population.

2 | Thinking About Electoral Expansion

The franchise sets the legal boundaries for voting participation. But, participation in politics is a multifaceted and broad phenomenon—surely involving more than the simple act of voting. Yet, the act of voting is the most commonly recognized and most basic measure of political participation. Inquiry into participation in this mode must begin with a consideration of the size and composition of the electorate, of who and what constitute the corps of eligible voters. Necessarily, this involves two considerations. The first is the formal or legal definition of the electorate. The second is the informal or behavioral categorization of which segments, in fact, usually do participate.

Suffrage Expansions

The story of the development of American suffrage, as in other Western democracies, is one of ever-increasing inclu-

sion. The Twenty-sixth Amendment to the U.S. Constitution,
which lowered the minimum voting age to eighteen, is but the
latest in a series of expansions of the electorate which have
composed the American political experience. Prior to the
liberalization of the age criterion, the major new inclusions to
the suffrage were the propertyless, Blacks, and women.

Initially, suffrage in America was a very limited affair, enjoyed only by propertied white males. Indeed, according to
Robert E. Lane, "immediately before the revolution, seven of
the thirteen colonies maintained an uncompromising landed
property qualification on voting, while the other six permitted
a person to substitute either evidence of personal property or a
tax payment as a prerequisite for admittance to the franchise." [1] The history of suffrage expansion in the first half of
the nineteenth century is the story of the relaxation of these
property and income qualifications for voting.

Following the emergence of virtually universal, white, male
suffrage, the removal of racial and ethnic barriers to voting
took place. According to Lane, one reason for the longer
retention of restrictive property, literacy, and residence requirements in the eastern states was the greater presence of
immigrants there. And with the removal of such requirements, direct restrictions on voting by naturalized Americans
were adopted.[2] Such restrictions as waiting two years after
becoming citizens before voting did not last long, in large
measure because they were not adopted in the western states.

The legal enfranchisement of Blacks has been a more tor-
tured and multistepped process. Prior to the Civil War, some
northern states restricted Black voting, while others did not.
In general, Black suffrage was enjoyed only where they were

1. Robert E. Lane, *Political Life* (New York: The Free Press, 1959),
p. 9.
2. *Ibid.* p. 13.

fewest in number, not unlike the situation in pre-1960 southern politics. Only in Maine, Massachusetts, New Hampshire,
Rhode Island, and Vermont did state constitutions not pro-
hibit their voting.[3] Blacks were also enfranchised in New
York if they owned real estate worth $250 or more. Slaves,
of course, could not vote. Following the Civil War, the problem of Black suffrage overall became a national issue. Southern Blacks were enfranchised by the Reconstruction Act of
1867, while the Fourteenth and Fifteenth amendments to the
U.S. Constitution in 1868 and 1870 forbade suffrage restriction on the basis of "race, color, or previous condition of
servitude." [4]

While some southern Blacks played a part in politics during the short period of Reconstruction, when southern whites
regained political control of their states following 1877, whatever Black suffrage had existed was quickly undone. Southern state constitutions were rewritten to accomplish this end
in language which did not directly conflict with the letter of
the law in the Fifteenth Amendment. And the U.S. Supreme
Court refused to respond to the spirit behind these new constitutions.[5] The slaves were emancipated but Blacks did not
become citizens. This situation prevailed well beyond the
mid-twentieth century. It was not until the civil rights legislation of the 1960s that the southern Black began to enjoy
the basic right of citizenship, the right to vote.

The enfranchisement of women was a great issue in the first
two decades of the twentieth century, culminating in 1920
with the adoption of the Nineteenth Amendment. Incidentally,

---

3. Donald R. Matthews and James W. Prothro, *Negroes and the New
Southern Politics* (New York: Harcourt, Brace & World, 1966), p. 13.
    4. *Ibid.*
    5. *Ibid.*, pp. 14–15.

in the early years of the republic, the notion of women casting ballots was so implausible that they had been inadvertently not excluded in the New Jersey constitutions of 1776 and 1797. After a few women actually tried to exercise their rights, the state legislators corrected their previous oversight.[6] The passage from the era of the "New Jersey correction" to the Nineteenth Amendment was marked by state initiative in granting women suffrage, beginning with the territory of Wyoming in 1869. Later, when Wyoming became a state in 1890, women suffrage was included in the state constitution. Altogether, three other western states granted this privilege in the nineteenth century. Undoubtedly, the joining of the Progressive movement with the women's movement contributed to the latter's success.[7]

It took a century and a half, therefore, before three kinds of barriers had been breached—those of property, race, and sex. Only the barrier of age remained. There was always an artificial quality to this barrier. The age of twenty-one as the threshold for civil majority owed its origin to medieval times. Obviously, the establishment of political majority at age eighteen does not remove the barrier of age; it merely lowers it. What is of immediate interest regarding this most recent change in the composition of the electorate is the rationale for it. The definition of the electorate is an index of prevailing political values and the conflicts of the time. Each of the previous expansions of the electorate is important in just this fashion. A brief review of some of these concerns for the past electoral expansions is helpful for considering some of the rationale behind the most recent electoral expansion, espe-

6. Lane, *op. cit.,* p. 16.
7. *Ibid.*

cially if there are parallels between the past and present concerns.

William H. Flanigan has suggested two general conditions conducive to electoral expansions. "In stable political systems the extension of suffrage will result from (1) a widely shared commitment to moral principles which entail further grants of suffrage, and (2) the expectation among political leaders that the newly enfranchised will support their policy preferences." [8]

The first major electoral expansion—the removal of property and tax-paying requirements for adult male suffrage—undoubtedly was a response to the evolving democratic ethos. The special condition facilitating the acceptance of this ethos was the western population expansion. Initially, restrictive voting qualifications were characteristic of the eastern states; the frontier regions were more liberal from the start. As Lane has observed, "Of all the new states admitted to the union only Tennessee imposed a property qualification upon the franchise, and after Mississippi (in 1817) no state entered the union with even a tax-paying qualification." [9] The practice of egalitarian politics was further reinforced by the absence of inherited class positions.

It is hard to ignore the fact that this democratic ethos constituted a moral principle of primary importance to all subsequent expansions of the electorate. This applies clearly to the enfranchisement of youth. Before the Twenty-sixth Amendment lowered the age criterion for all elections, it was lowered by federal statute for federal elections only, as per the Supreme Court's ruling on this legislation, December 21, 1970.

8. William H. Flanigan and Nancy H. Zingale, *Political Behavior of the American Electorate* (third edition, Boston: Allyn and Bacon, 1975), p. 9.
9. Lane, *op. cit.*, p. 12.

Despite his very real political apprehensions, President Nixon did not veto this legislation and instead signed it and expressed hope for a quick judicial test of its constitutionality. Given the democratic ethos, it would not have been realistic politically to veto such legislation, which had passed the Congress and seemingly had the approval of the public.

The moral principle celebrating popular participation in politics is deeply rooted in American political culture. This democratic ethos is articulated throughout society, from the lessons of high school civics to editorial comment in the mass media of communication. Moreover, it is reinforced by the celebration of competition in representative democratic political systems. This idealization of competition in the economic world was transferred in time to the political realm. C. B. Macpherson puts this very well:

> The claims of democracy would never have been admitted in the present liberal-democracies had those countries not got a solid basis of liberalism first. The liberal democracies that we know were liberal first and democratic later. To put this in another way, before democracy came in the Western world there came the society and the politics of choice, the society and politics of competition, the society and politics of the market. This was the liberal society and state.[10]

In retrospect, therefore, there is a logical and inexorable quality to the expansion of suffrage. In the long run, the fact of electoral expansion is eminently plausible. In reality, however, the path to electoral expansion has been anything but smooth. In fact, in the short run there has been one major regression—the constriction of the southern Black electorate around the end of the nineteenth and beginning of the twen-

10. C. B. Macpherson, *The Real World of Democracy* (London: Oxford University Press, 1966), p. 6.

tieth centuries. Noting the special and particular conditions attending electoral expansion means viewing such expansions in terms of their consequences for the distribution of power at a given point in time.

The case of female suffrage provides the clearest illustration of the argument that the expansion of suffrage owes much to the political needs of those with the power to grant or withhold it. Alan P. Grimes's analysis of the woman suffrage movement and the nativist forces behind it is a case in point.[11] The advocates of prohibition and immigration restriction also supported female suffrage, which they saw as a resource for their crusade. The European immigrations of the late nineteenth and early twentieth centuries had set the stage for a conflict of life-styles which dominated political consciousness in the first quarter of the twentieth century. This conflict is nowhere more clearly etched than in the conflict between "wet" and "dry" forces over prohibition. In this great cultural conflict the female vote became a Republican resource.[12] On one level the female vote was to have a "cleansing" effect on politics; on another level it would reinforce Republican electoral majorities as well. Thus, it is not accidental that women were enfranchised during the high tide of Republican ascendancy.

The enfranchisement of women, and that of southern Blacks, too, followed a period of intense social movements directed in large measure to this political right. This was less the case in the lowering of the age criterion for voting. While something of a student movement emerged in the 1960s, on elite and larger university campuses, its focus was largely on

11. Alan P. Grimes, *The Puritan Ethic and Women Suffrage* (New York: Oxford University Press, 1967).
12. *Ibid.,* p. 70.

United States involvement in the war in Southeast Asia, university complicity in the American military effort, and the assertion of student rights within the universities, rather than the direct political right of voting in elections.[13] In the early 1960s the student movement had participated in the burgeoning civil rights movement. While student political activity did reflect a policy commitment, and a liberal one at that, it had largely eschewed any consciousness of orthodox political means to these ends. Thus, in one sense, it can be said that this most recent expansion of the electorate took place despite the unconcern of students and, more generally, youth itself with suffrage. In another sense, of course, the very involvement of some segment of youth in politics, together with the sacrifices asked of some youth in the Vietnam war, was a powerful rationale for those legislators who argued for votes for youth. No doubt the known Democratic tendencies of young voters also had something to do with the fact that a Democratic-controlled Congress passed this legislation in advance of the re-election campaign of a Republican president. So while this idea had been on the political agenda in a minor way for at least two decades prior to its adoption, its ultimate acceptance is in large measure a response to the special social and political conditions of the 1960s. In this sense, therefore, the enfranchisement of youth was not unlike that of women earlier. Suffrage expansions have been furthered both by pragmatic and symbolic imperatives.

Political elites—specifically members of the Congress and state legislatures—led the way to the enfranchisement of youth. The consensus on this matter was something else for

13. For a reflection of this situation in survey data see Paul A. Beck and M. Kent Jennings, "The Case of the Reluctant Electorate," *Public Opinion Quarterly,* 33 (Fall, 1969), 370–79.

the population in general. For while public opinion polls consistently demonstrated approval for the youth suffrage, state referenda on the question were as consistently negative in outcome. To some extent this discrepancy reflects the choices of two different populations—the overall national population reflected in a national probability sample as compared to the more narrowly based population who actually participate in elections, especially in a state referendum vote. The more conservative response of those who actually do cast ballots has been demonstrated.[14] This discrepancy may also reflect the overall commitment to political egalitarianism, which is a dominant component of the American political culture, even by those who would reject it in the privacy of the voting booth. Such a disjuncture between the commitment to general principles and their specific manifestation is not unknown in American politics. Some three decades ago Gunnar Myrdal wrote about the "American dilemma"—the discrepancy between American beliefs on equality and human relations and their actual expression in the relations between the races.[15] More recently Lloyd Free and Hadley Cantril wrote about ideological conservatives and operational liberals—who can be the same persons. Here the discrepancy lies between being a conservative in the abstract and a liberal in terms of desired specific benefits produced by government.[16] A person might lament the influence of government on the individual but at the same time be the first to support federal social security programs.

14. Norman H. Nie and Sidney Verba, *Participation in America* (New York: Harper & Row, 1972), p. 284.

15. Gunnar Myrdal, *An American Dilemma* (New York: Harper, 1944).

16. Lloyd A. Free and Hadley Cantril, *The Political Beliefs of Americans* (New York: Simon and Schuster, 1968).

It is worth noting that popular rejection of electoral expansion has been a part of other suffrage liberalizations as well. Prior to the passage of the Fifteenth Amendment, referenda providing for Negro suffrage were rejected, as were referenda providing for woman suffrage prior to the passage of the Nineteenth Amendment.[17] Existing voters exhibit apprehensive anticipation of what havoc the newly enfranchised might wreak with the privilege. The real world of electoral expansion is caught between the cultural commitment to the symbol of a broader suffrage and the conservative tendencies of the established groups and interests. This discontinuity is a source of strain in the body politic.

Defining the Electorate:
Behavioral Considerations

The definition of the electorate has varied over time, although the overall trend has been toward liberalization. And this definition has been political in character, in the fullest sense of the term. The composition of the electorate has been subject both to the constraint of political power considerations and to the enduring values of the political culture. It is clear, therefore, that the formal definition of the electorate is only one dimension of an inquiry into political participation. The informal definition of the electorate must depend upon the findings of political behavior research, which provide us with an insight into the real world of electoral parameters. This latter consideration is important for any assessment of the potential and impact of the youth vote.

In general, there are three dimensions of orthodox political behavior. The first is voting participation. The second is the partisan direction of participation, or who and what is

17. Grimes, *op. cit.,* p. 21.

advantaged or disadvantaged by this participation. The third dimension consists of the attitude orientations and policy preferences, which impact upon the representative process and ultimately provide substantive meaning to the democratic political process. Indeed, the manner in which new currents of opinion affect the political parties is a major part of the story of the youth vote.

Richard M. Scammon and Ben J. Wattenberg have set forth the basic demographic parameters of voting participation more succinctly than anyone else: ". . . more than one of every three adults don't vote, and young people, poor people, and blacks are less likely to vote than the middle-aged, the wealthy, or whites." [18] In explaining these patterns, political behavior research has yielded two series of constraints—sociological and attitudinal—which merit notice. These constraints are analytically distinct, but also interdependent.

There is no dearth of literature to help explain political participation. The best and most useful summary treatments are those of Don R. Bowen,[19] William H. Flanigan,[20] Robert E. Lane,[21] and Lester W. Milbrath.[22] One of the basic facts of political participation is that it increases with socioeconomic status. More specifically, participation is a function of education. Socioeconomic status (SES) itself is a composite variable including elements of income, occupation, and edu-

18. Richard M. Scammon and Ben J. Wattenberg, *The Real Majority* (New York: Coward-McCann, Inc., 1970), p. 46.

19. Don R. Bowen, *Political Behavior of the American Public* (Columbus, Ohio: Charles E. Merrill, 1968).

20. William H. Flanigan and Nancy H. Zingale, *Political Behavior of the American Electorate* (third edition, Boston: Allyn and Bacon, 1975).

21. Robert E. Lane, *Political Life* (New York: The Free Press, 1959).

22. Lester W. Milbrath, *Political Participation* (Chicago: Rand McNally, 1965).

cation. It is this last component which, more than the other two, leads to higher rates of voting participation. One of the most consistently supported propositions in social science is that the more formal education a person has, the more likely he is to vote.

A second basic fact of voting participation is that it is very much a function of age. The participation rate for the youngest segment of the electorate has been consistently less than that for any other segment. Participation rates rise with age, reaching a plateau in late middle age and then declining in old age.[23]

These two generalizations on education and age that account for political participation touch directly on what may be expected of a "youth vote." However, they yield conflicting expectations regarding participation rates. The age variable alone suggests a lower rate of voting by the young; education suggests a relatively high rate of participation. Thus, any focus on only one of these variables would yield an incomplete expectation of the behavior of youth.

The decade of the 1960s was one of educational expansion and opportunity, particularly in higher education, which is reflected in U.S. Census Bureau comparisons of educational attainment in 1970 with 1960.[24] It is important to emphasize that it was still only a minority of those between

23. Angus Campbell, *et al., The American Voter* (New York: John Wiley, 1960), pp. 493–98. It should be noted that some recent research demonstrates that the decline in voting on the part of older persons may have been overstated in past research, that participation does not decline among the elderly if one corrects for SES and in particular for the education component of SES. See Sidney Verba and Norman H. Nie, *Participation In America* (New York: Harper & Row, 1972), ch. 9.

24. U.S. Bureau of the Census, *Current Population Reports,* Series P-20, No. 207, "Educational Attainment: March 1970" (Washington, D.C.: U.S. Government Printing Office, 1970).

eighteen and twenty years of age who benefited from this expansion. At the same time, however, it is also important to recognize that this education revolution did stamp the youth segment of the population in the 1960s in a manner different from younger persons in previous decades and, of course, older persons as well. Furthermore, Census Bureau estimates of voting participation with controls on *age* and *education* do demonstrate the very considerable impact of educational attainment on younger persons' voting participation. This is very clear in the following table, which presents 1964 data.

Table 2 | Voting Participation by Age and Education: 1964

Education	Per Cent Voters of Total Reported	
	21–24 years	*21 years and over*
All levels	52.2%	70.0%
Elementary, 0–7 years	17.6	51.6
Elementary, 8 years	24.9	67.4
High School, 1–3 years	33.7	65.9
High School, 4 years	55.4	76.5
College, 1–3 years	69.9	82.6
College, 4 years or more	78.9	88.2
Not Reported	26.5	36.8

SOURCE: U.S. Bureau of the Census, *Current Population Reports,* Series P-20, No. 143, "Voter Participation in the National Election: November 1964," Washington, D.C.: Government Printing Office, 1965.

Education has a startling interactive effect on the impact of age on participation. For while only a bit more than half of those twenty-one to twenty-four years of age voted in the 1964 election, a far different picture emerges with education controlled. In the 1964 presidential election, the voting participation rate for the college-graduate segment of the twenty-one- to twenty-four-year-old age group approached that of the

Table 3 | Reported Voter Participation of Persons 18 to 34 Years Old by School Enrollment Status and Age: 1972

School Enrollment Status and Age	Per Cent Reported Voted
Total Persons	
18 to 34 years	54.9%
18 to 20 years	48.3
21 to 24 years	50.7
25 to 29 years	57.8
30 to 34 years	61.9
Enrolled in School	
18 to 34 years	68.5
18 to 20 years	63.5
21 to 24 years	71.3
25 to 29 years	77.2
30 to 34 years	79.1
Not Enrolled in School	
18 to 34 years	54.0
18 to 20 years	39.7
21 to 24 years	47.4
25 to 29 years	58.0
30 to 34 years	63.1

SOURCE: U.S. Bureau of the Census, *Current Population Reports,* Series P-20, No. 253, "Voting and Registration in the Election of November 1972," Washington, D.C.: Government Printing Office, 1973.

college-educated segment of the entire population. Education has a far greater impact on the voting participation of the young than on older age groups.

The Census Bureau does not provide information demonstrating the interactive effect of age and education for voting participation in the years following 1964. Nevertheless, comparable information is available for the 1972 election and the same tendency appears again. Table 3 demonstrates that education has a considerable positive impact on the behavior of the young electorate. Voting participation in 1972 for the eighteen- to thirty-four-year-old population segment was estimated at 55 per cent overall but at 68 per cent for those enrolled in school. And among those aged eighteen to twenty, only 40 per cent voted. But, among the same age segment enrolled in school, voting participation reached 64 per cent.

While age and socioeconomic status are important constraints on voting participation, there are attitudinal constraints as well. In particular, the sense of uselessness, personal powerlessness, and inconsequence—in other words, personal alienation—is the major attitudinal constraint on political participation, especially for young people. And in the absence of a motivational factor, young people simply do not have the habits of participation or partisanship to sustain and direct political involvement.

Alienation is one of the grand concepts of sociological theory and is one of the central contributions of Karl Marx and Emile Durkheim. Its exploration has motivated much work but sustained less consensus regarding its meaning. Clearly, refinement of this much-used concept has been needed. To this end Melvin Seeman has differentiated five different meanings for this concept, alienation—powerlessness, meaninglessness, normlessness, isolation, and self-estrangement.[25] Not all of these meanings are relevant to political participation, especially the participation of youth. While the first three are relevant, the last two are not. The concepts powerlessness, meaninglessness, and normlessness closely approximate Leo Srole's work on the anomie scale.

25. Melvin Seeman, "On the Meaning of Alienation," *American Sociological Review*, 24 (December 1959), 783–91.

This instrument was devised to measure whether and to what extent a person feels that officials are unresponsive to him, that the social order is random and unpredictable, that one's personal situation in the world is hopeless, and other items.[26] Orientations such as these are held disproportionately by older and less well-educated persons.[27]

In the broadest sense, therefore, this attitudinal constraint on participation, whether it be called anomie, alienation, or cynicism, as Milbrath calls it,[28] taps an orientation of the self to politics and government. The major political consequence of this condition is a withdrawal from or reduced participation in politics. It is important to recall that this condition is inversely related to educational attainment.[29] Thus, with this attitudinal constraint, political behavior research offers a suggestion as to why higher educational attainment leads to increased political participation. In the past, education and alienation have been negatively correlated. The educated participated at higher rates because they were more efficacious and less alienated. But, there may well be a time-bound quality to these relationships as, increasingly, alienation is not the exclusive province of the less well-educated. The discovery of alienation among the educated young will be discussed in the following chapter.

The Decline in Voting Participation Since 1960

The behavioral definition of the electorate is but prologue to one of the most pressing concerns to researchers in po-

26. Lane, *op. cit.,* pp. 167–68.
27. *Ibid.,* p. 168.
28. Milbrath, *op. cit.,* p. 78.
29. *Ibid.,* p. 79.

litical behavior and theorists of the American political system—namely, the recent persistent decline in voting participation. Since 1960, when voting participation reached a twentieth-century high point, turnout rates have declined steadily. The most sizable recent decline occurred between 1968 and 1972, as the following table indicates. Turnout continued to decline in the 1976 presidential balloting.

Table 4 | Participation in Presidential Voting: 1920–72

1920	43.5%
1924	43.9
1928	51.9
1932	52.4
1936	56.9
1940	58.9
1944	56.0
1948	51.1
1952	61.6
1956	59.3
1960	62.8
1964	61.8
1968	60.9
1972	55.7

SOURCES: *Statistical Abstract of the United States,* 1974, 1971.

The history of electoral turnout in the twentieth century yields several general conditions for turnout. First, some combination of issue and candidate interest can sustain relatively high turnout rates. The elections of 1920 and 1924, the low watermarks of voting participation, were followed by the relatively stimulating candidacies of Alfred E. Smith and Franklin D. Roosevelt in 1928 and 1932. In later decades the candidate-oriented campaigns of Dwight D. Eisenhower in 1952 and John F. Kennedy in 1960 provided recent high points of electoral participation.

The issues of the New Deal program stimulated electoral participation during the 1930s, especially by the working class, which saw a clear stake in the success of this program and participated in greater than usual numbers. The decade of the 1930s was also a period of electoral realignment which predictably increased voting participation. It is surely the case that the contemporary decline in voting participation owes something to the attenuation of the older New Deal electoral alignment and the inability of the party system to assert a new electoral alignment.

A second general condition for turnout reflects the observation that a legally defined electoral expansion is followed by a decline in turnout when the new component of the electorate is not accustomed to the exercise of the franchise. Lane points to the decline in turnout that followed the enfranchisement of women.[30] It is easy to make the comparable assertion regarding the enfranchisement of youth prior to the 1972 election. Such an argument, however, would be too facile, and would have to include, at a minimum, some evidence of the turnout rates of the different population groups. It is unlikely that the sharp decline in electoral participation from 1968 to 1972 can be attributed solely or even largely to the inclusion of youth in the electorate. For while just under half of those aged eighteen to twenty years voted in 1972 (48.3 per cent), the decline in turnout overall reached 5.2 per cent. Moreover, both evidence and theory suggest that the effects of the education revolution would counter, in some measure, the admittedly dismal past record of participation by new and young voters. In addition, the decline in voting participa-

30. Lane, *op. cit.,* p. 22.

tion was in process prior to the recent electoral expansion. The twentieth century has consistently witnessed lower turn-out than the post-Civil War era of the nineteenth century, which was an emotionally charged period in which parties represented clearly opposed sectional interests.

The politics of economic class and sectional oppositions point to a third condition affecting turnout. Despite the evidence that the 1930s was an era of increased electoral turnout over the previous few decades, Lane observed that economic class issues and, more generally, nationalized electoral cleavages, both central to the New Deal realignment, generally show less electoral turnout than that for the era of sectional oppositions.[31] Lane suggests that the potential of full voting participation generated by economic class issues is hampered by the equivocal status of economic class appeals in American politics. The notion of economic *class* conflict does not rest comfortably within the American political culture, which has placed a greater emphasis on *individual* competition and conflict. Moreover, Lane adds, "For lower-class individuals, there is an implicit humiliation in acceptance of their relatively lower status, and hence a reluctance to participate in politics on a basis which emphasizes this lower status." [32]

While such an argument is plausible and worth noting, a more firmly grounded theory of political behavior points to the feeling of a lack of personal and political efficacy on the part of lower-status persons.[33] Relating feelings of efficacy to participation does not negate Lane's suggestion regarding the meaning of economic cleavage in American politics; indeed, it may contribute an additional dimension to our under-

31. *Ibid.,* p. 23.
32. *Ibid.*
33. Milbrath, *op. cit.,* pp. 56–57.

standing of it. In a politics increasingly charged by economic and/or group conflicts, those who stand to gain the greatest improvement in their lives through governmental action may suffer the greatest disillusionment by the gap between their expectation and reality.

Any assessment of the rate of voting participation in American politics must pause to consider the barrier of voting registration as a prelude to voting, or to follow the suggestion of Stanley Kelley, Jr., and his colleagues—"Putting First Things First." [34] It would be difficult to argue that the recent decline in voting participation results exclusively from the requirement of prior voter registration, inasmuch as the last few years have witnessed the greatest liberalization of registration requirements in this century, i.e., since their establishment. The Twenty-fourth Amendment to the U.S. Constitution, adopted in 1964, ended the poll tax as a prerequisite to voting, which had previously, in effect, disenfranchised many of the southern poor. Similarly, the use of literacy tests as a criterion for voter eligibility was ended by the Voting Rights Law of 1970. This, too, had its major impact on the South.

Two additional liberalizations of national consequence merit notice. Prior to 1970, the requirement of long-term residency for voter registration appeared to be the largest single impediment to a more complete participation in elections. The requirement of a one-year residency in a state was not uncommon. In 1970, Congress passed legislation reducing the residency requirement for voting in presidential elections to thirty days, and in March 1972 the U.S. Supreme Court declared unconstitutional long-term residency restric-

34. Stanley Kelley, Jr., Richard E. Ayres, and William G. Bowen, "Registration and Voting: Putting First Things First," *American Political Science Review*, 61 (June 1967), 359–79.

tions for voting in state and local elections. These legal developments, together with the rising educational levels in the population, should have resulted in higher levels of voting participation instead of the lower rates which actually occurred during the past decade.

The fact that voter participation has declined even after the passage of reform measures designed to facilitate the exercise of the franchise prompts consideration of alternative explanations for low turnout. An interesting and provocative alternative viewpoint is provided by Kevin P. Phillips and Paul H. Blackman, who argue that social and cultural factors are more important for turnout than any system of voter registration.[35] The importance and the character of the cultural bases for political behavior will be elaborated in chapter 4. For the moment it suffices to suggest that there is evidence on both sides of the question. On balance there seems to be little doubt but that prior registration is a crucial variable for voting participation. However, what needs analysis is whether a separate set of factors affects registration independent of voting participation.

Political scientists have long known about the importance of prior voter registration in influencing the size of electoral turnout. In 1924, Charles E. Merriam and Harold G. Gosnell demonstrated that "there were three times as many adult citizens who could not vote because they had failed to register as there were registered voters who had failed to vote." [36] More recently, Stanley Kelley and his associates demonstrated ". . . the extremely strong relationship between the date at

35. Kevin P. Phillips and Paul H. Blackman, *Electoral Reform and Voter Participation* (Washington, D.C.: American Enterprise Institute for Public Policy Research, 1975).
36. Kelley, *op. cit.,* p. 359.

which registration rolls are closed and the percentage of voting age that is registered." [37] Aside from the necessity of making two trips to the polls before casting one's first ballot, the major mechanism by which registration hindered voting was the necessity of a person making a decision to vote long before the excitement of the election campaign itself.

The issue of the relationship between prior voter registration and voting participation is complicated by historical factors. In the larger context of centuries, rather than decades, however, it would be hard to ignore the relationship between registration and voting. The last quarter of the nineteenth century, which witnessed turnout rates of more than 75 per cent of the eligible electorate, was also a period devoid of voter registration requirements. The sharp decline in voting participation at the turn of the twentieth century was accompanied by the establishment of prior voter registration in many of the states.[38] But the adoption of registration laws was not uniform across the states. At the same time, the decline in voting participation was similar in both registration and nonregistration counties and states.[39] In this situation, the decline in voter participation owed more to the political factor of the reduction of the scope of competition for the presidency than to the legal factor of registration laws.

Notwithstanding the conflicting evidence and argument on registration and voting, a very general consensus prevails that the American system of voter registration is *a* major, if not *the* major, obstacle to higher voter participation rates. It is a

---

37. *Ibid.,* p. 367.

38. Besides Kelley's article, see Jerrold G. Rusk, "The Effect of the Australian Ballot Reform on Split Ticket Voting: 1876–1908," *American Political Science Review,* 63 (December 1970), 1220–238.

39. Phillips and Blackman, *op. cit.,* p. 51.

system sustained by private initiative and the voluntary efforts of not overly ambitious party organizations. By contrast, in Europe, voter registration is a government responsibility. The higher voter participation of the electorate in Europe may be attributed, in part, to the ease and automatic character of voter registration. Similarly, in the United States, higher rates of voter participation have been recorded in those states in which it was easier to register and stay registered. For example, voter participation rates in Idaho stand at between 70 and 80 per cent of the potential electorate, as compared to much lower rates elsewhere in the nation. In Idaho, however, voter registration has been extremely easy. Registration is permitted until two days before the general election and may be accomplished even by mail. Furthermore, the registration stands unless the vote is not cast in any election for a period of eight years.[40]

It is clear that registration and voting are two distinct steps in the American election system and that the best single predictor of voting participation is prior voter registration. This relationship holds even if there are cultural and political factors which mitigate against both registration and voting itself. In any event, voter registration has been an important component of recent presidential campaigns, especially Democratic ones. This was clear in John F. Kennedy's campaign in 1960, in which direction of the registration campaign was entrusted to U.S. Representative Frank Thompson of New Jersey. The Kennedy strategists held that of 40 million unregistered voters in 1960, 70 per cent would vote Democratic.[41] Whether or not reality matched expectation in 1960,

40. John J. Patrick and Allen D. Glenn, *The Young Voter* (Washington, D.C.: National Council for the Social Studies, 1972), pp. 28–29.
41. T. H. White, *The Making of the President 1960* (New York: New American Library, 1967), p. 282.

a similar expectation, this time directed toward the potential youth vote, was voiced early in McGovern's 1972 presidential campaign. Frederick S. Dutton, a McGovern registration strategist, expected nearly three-fourths of youth to vote Democratic and urged a massive registration campaign. In this case, reality clearly fell short of expectation. As early as July 22, 1972, the Gallup Poll reported that a massive registration campaign would benefit only Nixon.[42]

Yet, clearly there was reason for McGovern to consider the importance of registering the young, up to a point, for he was supported disproportionately by the educated young. And education related to registration in the same manner as to voting more generally. McGovern's problem was that those who could be expected to vote for him were registered already.

The impact of education on registration emerges clearly in the table on page 52.

As of August 1972, 67 per cent of the college student segment of the population under thirty was registered while only 47 per cent of the noncollege segment under thirty was registered. Of all the variables considered, education provides the largest differential for registration. Obviously, this uneven rate of registration, together with McGovern's disproportionate support among the college young, especially the graduate student segment, is why a mass registration effort among all the young would have been counterproductive. Thus, it is not surprising that the Gallup Poll revealed that while the then presently registered young favored McGovern, the unregistered young favored Nixon.[43]

Not only is the importance of educational attainment important in a cross-sectional analysis of participation, but its

42. *Philadelphia Inquirer,* July 23, 1972, p. 20.
43. *Ibid.*

Table 5 | Percentage Registered for Different Categories of the Under-30 Age Population, August 1972

Total	54%
College	67
Noncollege	47
Men	54
Women	54
South	51
Non-South	55
Whites	54
Non-whites	57
Republicans	58
Democrats	60
Independents	49

SOURCE: *Gallup Opinion Index,* Report No. 86 (August 1972).

effect is also apparent in an analysis over time of voting participation. The comparison of participation rates within education categories for 1968 and 1972 is very revealing. As Table 6 demonstrates, participation rates between 1968 and 1972 declined disproportionately within the less educated segments of the entire population and were relatively stable for the college-graduate segment. A major implication of these data is that the decline in voting participation surely would have been sharper in the absence of recent gains in educational attainment. Admittedly, what may have happened here is that the less educated segments may have had a champion in 1968 in the person of George C. Wallace, which stimulated their participation that year. In 1972 such a champion was not available to them in the general election.

Table 6 | Voter Participation by Education: 1968, 1972

Education	Percentage Reporting Voting		Difference:
	1968	*1972*	*1968–1972*
0–4 years	38.4%	33.0%	5.4%
5–7 years	52.4	44.3	8.1
8 years	62.4	55.2	7.2
9–11 years	61.3	52.0	9.3
12 years	72.5	65.4	7.1
College, 1–3 years	78.4	74.9	3.5
College, 4 years	83.1	82.3	0.8
College, 5 years +	85.7	85.6	0.1

SOURCE: U.S. Bureau of the Census, *Current Population Reports,* Series P-20, No. 253, "Voting and Registration in the Election of November 1972" (U.S. Government Printing Office, Washington, D.C., 1973).

The Consequences of Electoral Expansion

The extension of suffrage to different classes of persons in the population is of consequence for the rules of political conduct, the character of public discourse, the public policies and values of the society, and the fortunes of some politicians. It is obvious that in a short period of years southern politics has lost much of its distinctive stamp following the enfranchisement of Blacks. The race-baiting rhetoric of old-guard southern politicians has passed and Blacks are being elected to office throughout the South. There has also been a decline in the saliency of the race issue as a basis for cleavage in southern politics. This decline accounts, in part, for the popularity of Jimmy Carter over George C. Wallace in the 1976 presidential primary elections in the southern states.

Great political change also followed major changes in the composition of the electorate in the nineteenth century. The decline of the Federalist party after 1800 owed something to the expansion of the electorate, which did away with property requirements for voting. Later, at the end of the century, the Republican party was excluded from the South by the contraction of suffrage.[44]

Joel H. Goldstein has provided a typology of the ways the extension of suffrage can affect the political balance of power.[45] He categorizes the effects of suffrage extensions in terms of *reinforcing, reflecting,* and *reforming* outcomes. The reinforcement effect occurs when the new suffrage class supports the party which enfranchises it. The reflecting effect occurs when this class divides along the same lines in the same manner as already exist in the electorate. The reforming effect refers to support for a previously minor or nonexistent party.[46]

In the case of the most recent suffrage extension, it is in the direction of this third, or reforming, direction that the youth vote will be of greatest consequence. This does not necessarily imply support for minor or new parties, as the typology suggests. Instead, its impact may be felt in altered political appeals, in the politicalization of demands and perspectives which ultimately will be of consequence for the ideational and group bases of the parties, and possibly for the institution of party itself. For it is the argument of this essay that the atti-

44. William H. Riker, *Democracy in the United States* (New York: Macmillan, 1953), p. 41 and ch. 2, "Suffrage in the United States," *passim.*
45. Joel H. Goldstein, "The Effects of the Adoption of Woman Suffrage: Sex Differences in Voting Behavior—Illinois 1914–1921," unpublished Ph.D. dissertation, University of Chicago, 1973.
46. *Ibid.,* p. 32.

tudes and political orientations of contemporary young persons stand apart from those of older generations and that this is of consequence for the party system. The political patterns of youth are not, and will not become, a carbon copy of those of their parents. The literature on voting behavior which led to the expectation of minimal impact on the part of youth is simply not appropriate for gauging the present and future course of American politics.

In the short run there will be considerable strain as generational groups oppose each other from different stances. Ultimately, however, there will be convergence, consequent to the aging of these new generations together with the modification of establishment postures. The role of common symbols in a mass society and the symbolic appeal of youth contribute to this ultimate homogenization. The dynamics of this process, however, are surely radically different from those postulated in the classic studies of American voting behavior.

3 | Modern Society

Any account of the political behavior of youth, and of the impact of youth in American politics, must begin with an understanding of the character of modern society. For the rapid change in behavioral patterns, in juxtaposition to the relative stability and conservatism of political and governmental institutions, is a major source of discontinuity. This discontinuity contributes to the alienation epidemic that is rampant today.

To set the inquiry at the societal level also allows the interpreter to focus on all ages, not merely youth. It would be myopic and a mistake to deal with changes in the orientations and patterns of youth in recent years and to ignore similar changes in other sectors of society. Nevertheless, a special concern with youth is justified in that youth reflect disproportionately the changing currents of opinion in society.

In this respect, the young and the educated, especially the educated young, are important as vehicles of innovation in society.

The argument of this chapter, and indeed the entire essay, is that it is necessary to come to terms with the evolution of society and its implications for things political in order to make sense of voting behavior patterns. As the previous chapter demonstrated, the definition of suffrage itself is an index to societal values.

The growing lack of commitment to established political institutions and processes on the part of the young results from the growing discontinuity between social and political evolution. This discontinuity is the outcome of the clash of the rapidly evolving social and cultural realms with the relative stability of the political institutions and majority opinion. Change comes more quickly to society than to its political institutions, which by definition are relatively impervious to change.

This rapid societal evolution is not uniquely American; it is the process of modernization everywhere. Student protests and political cynicism are worldwide phenomena. The major policy implication of this insight is that the disjuncture and discontinuity is situated too deeply to be ameliorated by reforms that are conventional and routine.

Modern Society

As a type of society, the "modern" differs from the "traditional" in several important respects. Modern societies place great emphasis on the ethos of individualism and egalitarianism. These principles are elaborated in the importance of the nuclear family and the emphasis on status by achievement rather than ascription. Necessarily, education is a valued component of the modern experience and is a source of training for the technological and bureaucratic employment sectors that are dominant today.

The passage from traditional to modern societies is marked by a very special evolution in social relations. In particular, as societies become modern, they become increasingly complex through the general processes of differentiation and individuation. The individual person becomes relatively autonomous and bears, in large measure, the responsibility for his own self-development.

Paradoxically, modern society, which celebrates individual advancement and the pursuit of opportunity, also restricts the behavior of different age groups. The segregation and isolation of older persons is one expression of this restriction. The marginal and dependent status of youth is another.

Two characteristics in particular are shared by both the aged and the young—their economic nonutility and their segregation in residential and cultural settings. In a more traditional milieu, both the aged and young were integral components of economic productivity. If this setting was a rural one, in an enterprise combining home and commercial economy, division of labor *within* the family unit contributed to the economic well-being of the entire unit. Aged parents were an asset in the tasks of the home, which may have been the patriarch's in the first place, while children, too, were an asset in the tasks of the field and home. Indeed, the productivity of the enterprise was sustained by the contributions of the younger generation. With the loss of their economic utility in modern settings, children became economic burdens and then ultimately human "pets" for the gratification of the emotional needs of parents.

In a different but analogous setting, the immigrant family, the different members worked in separate enterprises outside the family, while often living in the same domicile or close by, and contributed to the material sustenance of aged parents. The extended family was still a reality, although a lessening one. Similarly, in the developing polities of the third world today it is not uncommon for both parents to work in the fields or factories away from home, leaving the care of their offspring to an older generation. The ultimate development of this tendency away from intergenerational dependence may well exist in present society, with both parents away at work in their professions, leaving the child with his contemporaries in a day-care center.

In the last portion of the twentieth century, America has moved away from past models of intergenerational interdependence in many important respects. Industrialization, technology, and relative affluence have rendered nonviable the persistence of the extended family as the major basis of social organization. More people are living longer now, in both helpless states requiring institutional care and in good health and relative financial independence. Again, the generations exist apart in the modern experience.

The consequence of these tendencies is that in two important respects social integration has weakened. The decline of the extended family has yielded the nuclear family. In turn the position of children in the new family structure is a constrained and limited one. Families are less integrated into the fabric of society and children are less integrated into the complete realm of family life.

Other implications of the nuclear family have been discussed by Kenneth Keniston.[1] According to his argument, the new division of labor in the twentieth-century American family left to the mother almost exclusively the parental role and

1. Kenneth Keniston, *The Uncommitted* (New York: Dell, 1970), pp. 23–37, 238–69.

to the father the producer role, usually compelling the father's absence from the home for the entire day. While this pattern is being challenged today by the movement for women's and men's liberation, it is still the dominant norm of social organization.

The major consequence of this role specialization was an inordinate dependency of the child on the mother. While psychologists claim that this pattern is not without its beneficial consequences—specifically for the development of the motivation to achieve, which is traced to maternal encouragement and support—it represents potential problems for the political order. The intense identity of the young child with the mother and the possible concomitant scorn of the father, according to Keniston, can leave a residue of unresolved conflicts extending into adulthood.[2] Similarly, Neil J. Smelser suggests a theorized but unproved notion that, when the father left the home for the job, some of his economic authority in the home left to a certain degree as well.[3] The need to disparage, attack, and reject the authority figure in the family—usually the male—can also be expressed by an attack on and rejection of other authority figures in society. From this perspective, the development of a youthful cynicism about politics and government is a very easy step. Despite this plausibility, however, empirical studies have failed to reveal any evidence of political rebellion among young people.[4]

In the post-World War II era, the state of dependency did

2. *Ibid.*, pp. 47–48.
3. Neil J. Smelser, "The Modernization of Social Relations," in Myron Weiner (ed.), *Modernization* (New York: Basic Books, 1966), ch. 8.
4. M. Kent Jennings and Richard G. Niemi, "The Transmission of Political Values from Parent to Child," *American Political Science Review,* 62 (March 1968), p. 171.

not end for American youth with the passing of childhood. Dependency dominated the second and third decades of life with the extension of schooling. James S. Coleman has written, "As the labor of children has become unnecessary to society, school has been extended to them." [5] While cries of irrelevance and tedium have recently emerged from increasing numbers of the high school segment of the population, the situation of the college and post-graduate student is even more acute. The strains of delayed career entry, in addition to the very real uncertainty of career choice for many, together with the financial cost of extended schooling, all point to the crystallization of an outlook characteristic of youth. Indeed, the very opportunity of education may well be the nemesis of this generation in that higher education carries with it a commitment to achievement and advancement that is not always supported by the reality of economic opportunity.

Notwithstanding the great importance of the model of the nuclear family in any understanding of modern society, this model is being compromised in important respects. The trend toward the society of single parents and day-care centers points to the decline of the nuclear family as a source of stable nurture. Even within conventional nuclear families, the pressures upon educated mothers to find meaningful activity outside the home and family result in lessened attention to parental tasks. Yet, through all of this there is a theme of continuity that is consistent with the character of modern society. For the autonomy of the family unit is being succeeded by the autonomy of the individual. But this celebration of the individual and his rights has had a counter-celebration. A quest for integration by some young moderns

5. James S. Coleman, *Youth: Transition to Adulthood* (Chicago: University of Chicago Press, 1974), p. vii.

has led to a resurgence of the popularity of crafts, communes, and religious cults.

The problem of individualism has been considered by many social theorists. In particular, two major intellectual constructs confront the meaning of extreme individualism, both for the person and for society. Both David Riesman's *The Lonely Crowd* [6] and William Kornhauser's *The Politics of Mass Society* [7] analyze the autonomy characteristic of extreme individualism and its behavioral consequences. The perspectives of both theorists converge on one major attribute of the modern individual—his quest to conform. For Riesman this conformity is expressed in terms of the "other-directed's" incessant search for the approval of others in matters of taste and culture. One's peers become the relevant others from whom approval is sought. For Kornhauser conformity is also an outcome, but is expressed in terms of the individual's capacity for mobilization into mass movements. Since both analyses deal with "ideal types" they necessarily represent reality in an imperfect manner. Yet, the tendencies expressed in modern society approach sufficiently these types and thereby validate their utility. This is especially the case among the young and the educated.

According to Riesman, "What is common to all the other-directed people is that their contemporaries are the source of direction for the individual—either those known to him or those with whom he is indirectly acquainted, through friends and through the mass media." [8] For such a person the cues

6. David Riesman, *The Lonely Crowd* (abridged edition, New Haven: Yale University Press, 1969), originally published in 1950.

7. William Kornhauser, *The Politics of Mass Society* (New York: The Free Press, 1959).

8. Riesman, *op. cit.,* p. 21.

to behavior are external to the family and may be found in the new and unconventional. In such a society tradition is no longer a limiting social state. Paradoxically, however, not all external and strange sources are sought after by the other-directed young as sources of cues. Instead, conformity to one's peers is the dominant expression of other direction.

The Riesman characterization of the emerging social type, the "other-directed," can be understood as an indictment of the consequences of extreme individualism. For what is lacking in the "other-directed" is the integration with other generations or a clear internal sense of identity and goals, as was the case for the "tradition-directed" and "inner-directed" types. The basic problem of the "other-directed" is his lack of identity and his need to compensate for this in finding it in the approval of others. A tendency toward similarity of opinion and behavior is the result.

Although writing from a different perspective and tradition, Kornhauser's theory reaches a similar position. The individual in the mass society is atomized, unconnected to other persons. He lacks any meaningful existence in groups. His expression of conformity is in the mass movement, in that artificial tie which replaces the missed integrated existence.

The world of mass movements is characterized by rigid adherence to both dogma and the charismatic leader. It is an inherently unstable world. The society lacking an infrastructure of intermediate associations and a plurality of loyalties can experience rapid and unpredictable mobilization. Although Kornhauser's analysis, like Riesman's, is in terms of ideal types, there are empirical referents which correspond in some manner to the types. Thus, American party politics can be characterized in terms of the declining commitment to the established party institutions and the increased importance of movement politics. This does not imply that the outcome for American politics need approximate at all that of Kornhauser's mass society, which was totalitarianism. At the same time, however, this need not detract from the utility of Kornhauser's insights and appreciation of the dynamics of mass society.

Both the Riesman and Kornhauser analyses imply an important paradox—the unacceptability of extreme, atomized individualism. Conformity succeeds individuality. To be sure, there are major differences in the analyses. Riesman's "other-directed" conform to the peer group while Kornhauser's mass man loses himself in the broader mass movement. Moreover, there is no implication that conformity is the exclusive province of the young. All age groups seek the psychic gratification of identification with and support from those of similar life situation and opinion. Thus, the dynamics of youth are not dissimilar from those governing the rest of society. However, the specific focus of the social groups may differ, and rates of susceptibility to innovation may differ, thereby making worthwhile concern with youth. Ultimately, it is through the study of youth that we become sensitive to problems affecting society in general.

Alienation

No one monolithic pattern characterizes the political behavior of youth. The image of this behavior varies with the segment of youth under consideration, as well as with the perspective of the viewer. Accordingly, for some viewers, youth's participation is nonparticipation, or apathy. Lower voting participation rates of young first voters are cited in support of this assertion. For other viewers, the characteristic pattern of youth is that of active and nonroutine participation.

The student demonstrations and sit-ins of the 1960s are a case in point. What both behavioral patterns share is a repudiation of orthodox, conventional political behavior, i.e., voting behavior. In two important respects these patterns are typical responses to the modernity that includes the rejection of traditional authority and the adoption of the attitudinal condition of alienation.

Modern society emphasizes the rational, the efficient, and the secular. Each of these emphases contributes to the rejection of traditional authority that is characteristic of society today, not only in America but elsewhere. Former symbols of authority such as religion, parents, and educational institutions no longer hold the obedience and influence they once did. Instead, the individual stands alone to question, to structure, and to create meaning for his own life. This is not without its benefits, largely in terms of the individual's challenge of more opportunity for autonomy and self-development than ever existed before.

These tendencies in society have been compounded by political factors as well. Government and officialdom have never before been held in such low esteem. The sources of this disillusionment are obvious. The Democratic administrations of the 1960s held forth the promise of accomplishments, both on the domestic front, as in the war on poverty, and on the foreign front, such as Vietnam. These expectations were dashed in the urban conflagrations of 1967 and 1968 and the seemingly interminable and useless Vietnam war. Subsequently, the forced resignation of Richard Nixon from the presidency and the realization of the extent of corruption in his administration have contributed mightily to the rejection of traditional authority. The recent combination of inflation and recession, in turn, has indicted the government for failure to fulfill the second most important function of government: to provide for the common welfare. For many victims of urban crime, and for the larger group fearful of becoming its victims, the first function of government, the maintenance of domestic tranquility, has failed fulfillment also.

These trends give reason enough for the individual to feel some sense of estrangement, of separation between his orientations and values and those of the society and polity. Yet, even more, such separation is implied by the process of modernization itself, as social theorists have long indicated. These theorists have concurred on a term for this condition—alienation. As Irving Louis Horowitz has written:

> The word "alienation" implies an intense separation—from objects in a world; from other people; and from ideas about the world held by other people. It might be said that the synonym of alienation is "separation" while the precise antonym of the word is "integration." [9]

Thus, even if recent events such as Watergate and social unrest had not occurred, the dynamics of modernization would have led to alienation.

The two major dimensions of alienation are the sociocultural and the political. The former refers to separation from the dominant values and purposes of society. The latter refers to a disidentification with, indeed a repudiation of, the political institutions and officers of the polity. This is of consequence for political behavior. Alienation is a general condition which antecedes both hyperparticipation in and withdrawal from political behavior. David C. Schwartz' pioneering revisionist theory of alienation relates alienation,

9. Irving Louis Horowitz, *Foundations of Political Sociology* (New York: Harper & Row, 1972), p. 557.

among other variables, to these very different political behaviors:

> Political alienation is typically associated with basic behavioral
> orientations to politics other than conformity; alienated people
> are far less likely to be conformists than are the nonalienated.
> The specific political behavior orientation which a given
> alienated person is likely to select is dependent upon his social
> status, his personality and his political attitudes. Alienated
> people who are upper-class, energetic and secure of their
> psychological, economic and political well-being tend to prefer
> active modes of expressing their alienation and to be reformist
> or revolutionary in their orientations. Those who are of lower
> SES, less angry, less energetic and less invulnerable to reper-
> cussions in the economy, polity or psyche tend to adopt more
> passive orientations to the polity, to withdraw or to be
> ritualists.[10]

It bears noting that Schwartz' association of alienation with
nonconformity refers to the rejection of established political
routines. There is no necessary inconsistency between conformity to the peer group, which is a characteristic response
to modern society, and nonconformity to the larger society
and polity. Indeed, it is very much the case that, in modern
society, nonconformity is expressed from a generational rather
than an individual basis.

From these perspectives on modern society it is possible to
suggest that a critical stance regarding authority follows logically the attitude of alienation. The use of the term "big
government" as a contemporary political indictment reflects
this mood. One of Schwartz' major arguments and findings
was that this attitude is no longer confined to the lower SES

10. David C. Schwartz, *Political Alienation and Political Behavior*
(Chicago: Aldine, 1973), p. 159.

segments of the population but is widespread, especially among elite segments. Similarly, the unexpectedly rapid diffusion of new values and orientations from elite college students to other college students, and to all younger persons, has been documented by Daniel Yankelovich.[11] These trends speak both to the utility of the model of mass society and to modern society itself as a force productive of alienation.

The political behavior of youth, and older generations, becomes more intelligible in the context of modern society. Modernity is a process and a system of social relations. It is also a value system with a commitment that the present is better than the past and the future will be better than the present. When society's return on its members' investment in this belief is increasingly meager, this sponsors alienation. But because of changing patterns of educational attainment, this alienation from the political system finds expression less in terms of unconcern and apathy and more in rejection of traditional patterns and openness to nonroutine political participation.

Alienation as a Political Resource

The focus of this new nonroutine participation suggests that youth be viewed as a resource for change in politics. This is a logical conclusion to the widely held generalization that youth are disproportionately susceptible to change and that alienation is the condition of modern man. These twin generalizations suggest consideration of an interpretation which holds that it is alienation which furthers social and political change. Thus, far from viewing alienation as a pathologic

11. Daniel Yankelovich, *The New Morality: A Profile of American Youth in the 70's* (New York: McGraw-Hill, 1974).

condition of modern society, it may be appropriate to view it instead as an important dynamic in social and political evolution.

Of course, not all of change should be viewed in a positive manner. Indeed, much that is subsumed by this broad and nearly ubiquitous concept of alienation has been destructive to the individual personality and to the political system. The traditional picture of the condition of alienation is largely one of this sort. The immersion of the alienated into the mass movement and totalitarianism is a dominant theme in social theory. Traditionally, the social basis of alienation was perceived to be among the less well-educated and the petit bourgeois. But, with the recognition of the pervasiveness of alienation and of its presence among economic and educated elites came an alternative understanding of the consequences of alienation. The energizing behavior of Schwartz' upper-class alienated is a case in point. These new alienated are akin to the alienated that Keniston discovered among elite college students. And these elite alienated were the ones who took seriously the values of the American democratic creed and repudiated the disjuncture between the creed and reality. Alienated such as these expressed the conscience of American politics.

This recognition of the positive aspect of alienation has its counterpart in Joseph Gusfield's incisive insight into the character and consequences of mass society.[12] Far from viewing mass society as a threat to democratic forms, Gusfield perceived it as a liberating condition from the heavy weight of the status quo. In other terms, a society that is

12. Joseph R. Gusfield, "Mass Society and Extremist Politics," *American Sociological Review,* 27 (February 1962), 19–30.

characterized by innovation is one that is not tied to tradition and is one in which groups and individuals can be mobilized readily. Thus, there is a correspondence between the structure of mass society and the human condition of alienation. Moreover, change itself is not alien to mass society. The reformist orientation toward politics on the part of some of such a society's youth is then neither strange nor unpredictable. Youth are a vehicle for change in American politics because of the dynamics of modernity.

4 | Political Socialization and Political Culture

The patterned activities that characterize social collectivities result from the process of socialization. Whether one's actions take place at home, at work, in a religious society, or in the society of citizens of which one is part, if these actions are routine and predictable they owe much to the process of socialization. Indeed, the existence of any social collectivity or society, and the character of that society, owes a great deal to the fact of socialization and the kind of socialization that exists.

Political socialization concerns the inculcation of those behaviors, orientations, and values that are relevant politically. Any concern with youth in politics necessarily concerns political socialization. As the newer members of society, the socialization of youth to politics is the mechanism by which societies are shaped and by which they persist. Socialization is also the dynamic by which the generations of man relate to one another, controlling in some measure the pattern and character of social evolution.

Margaret Mead has identified three patterns of this socialization—the "postfigurative, in which children learn primarily from their forebears, cofigurative, in which both children and adults learn from their peers, and prefigurative, in which adults learn also from their children." [1] One thing is very clear. While there may be ambiguity regarding whether American culture is cofigurative or prefigurative, it is surely not postfigurative. And therein lie implications for the kind of society and polity that may exist. A major prop for the notion of minimal impact of youth in politics was that they would not be very different from their parents. This assumption depended upon a postfigurative model of socialization, an assumption which is less than completely viable. For one of the major implications of modern society is the importance of the peer group in the socialization process. Moreover, the broad appeal of youth in American culture suggests that not only do the new generations seek cues and approval from their peers, but the culture of older generations is not untouched by that of the young.

The past dominant model of political socialization has emphasized the intergenerational continuity of political orientations and the stability of the political culture. Clearly, this model is less appropriate today. In times of accelerating social and economic change and clashes between former and present political orientations, socialization, or the way values and behavior are learned, reflects and expresses these changes. Ultimately, looking at political socialization can be profitable

1. Margaret Mead, *Culture and Commitment* (Garden City, New York: Doubleday, 1970), p. 1.

in understanding the bases, character, and dynamics of both stability and change.

Socialization perspectives are especially important in analyzing the political behavior of youth because of the intimate relation between political socialization and political culture. More generally, political culture is *the* foundation for political behavior. According to Kenneth P. Langton, "Political socialization, in the broadest sense, refers to the way society transmits its political culture from generation to generation." [2] Early studies of political socialization were dominated by inquiry into the impact of the family on political orientations. The usual finding was that there was a positive impact; voting behavior and party identification were handed down from parent to child. Indeed, socialization into the parents' political party was established more closely than in other dimensions of political life. Thus, Herbert H. Hyman suggested that "the socialization of the individual into a *party* is a much more direct process than the socialization of the logically congruent area of ideology." [3] Bernard Berelson and his associates particularly noted the strong partisan connection between the generations, finding ". . . four out of five with Republican fathers voted Republican in 1948, and two out of three with Democratic fathers voted Democratic even in this Republican town." [4] The more recent research of M. Kent Jennings and Richard G. Niemi refine the dimensions of political life and conclude that, again, it was in the realm of

2. Kenneth P. Langton, *Political Socialization* (New York: Oxford University Press, 1969), p. 4.

3. Herbert H. Hyman, *Political Socialization* (New York: The Free Press, 1959), p. 56.

4. Bernard R. Berelson, Paul F. Lazarsfeld, and William N. McPhee, *Voting* (Chicago: University of Chicago Press, 1954), pp. 88–89.

party identification that the strongest correspondence between parent and child occurred.[5]

For a variety of reasons, the model of intergenerational continuity is less than appropriate. First, it is increasingly apparent that the orientations of youth represent a generational change rather than a stage in the life cycle. Second, the antiparty ethos of the new independents represents a repudiation of the basic ingredient for intergenerational partisan continuity. Third, the shift in the political culture from support to nonsupport of political institutions similarly contributes against the continuity of political attachments. Fourth, the decline in familial socialization together with its replacement by peer group and societal socialization dynamics mitigate against political continuity. These four factors are the essential reasons to expect a different pattern of behavior by youth.

During the decade of the 1960s, one interpretation of American voting behavior was dominant, that of *The American Voter.* [6] This seminal study documented a high degree of correspondence between the respondents' party identification and that recalled for their parents.[7] Furthermore, the authors of *The American Voter* found that although persons just entering the electorate were more likely than older citizens to identify themselves as independents rather than partisans, they became partisans with the passage of time.[8] From the perspective of *The American Voter,* therefore, much political behavior depended upon one's position in the life cycle.

5. M. Kent Jennings and Richard G. Niemi, "The Transmission of Political Values From Parent to Child," *American Political Science Review,* 62 (March 1968).

6. Angus Campbell, *et al., The American Voter* (New York: John Wiley, 1960).

7. *Ibid.,* p. 147.

8. *Ibid.,* p. 161.

While these findings were true and appropriate for the decade of the 1950s, later research suggests a different picture.
Gerald M. Pomper has documented the decline in partisan
correspondence between parent and child in 1968 and 1972.[9]
Furthermore, the independent identification of new voters
did not return to routine partisan patterns in a few years, as
would be expected by the model of the life-cycle pattern of
partisan affiliation. The rise of the new independents will be
discussed further in chapter 5. In general, party identification has become a less and less reliable guide to political
behavior. This change is itself a major alteration of the political environment and a reflection of the changed saliency
of the political party institution in contemporary society. This
decline in the traditional character and impact of party identification also reflects the attenuation of the cultural commitment to party as well as the rise of extrafamilial agents of
socialization.

Political socialization is essentially political learning. It is
possible to distinguish analytically and empirically three different sources of this learning—the *family,* the *peer group*
and *schools,* and the *societal.* These are not mutually exclusive, either in effects or in co-occurrence. What is important
is that each of these has particular consequences for the character of society and its culture. Necessarily, this includes politics as well.

Different patterns of learning predominate at different stages
of personal development and at different junctures in the socialization process. The child's ability to acquiesce to authority owes much to the model of family life he knows. Furthermore, as David Easton and Jack Dennis suggest, "His early
experience of government is analogous to his early experience

9. Gerald M. Pomper, *Voters' Choice* (New York: Dodd, Mead, 1975),
pp. 24–25.

of the family in that it evolves in an initial context of highly acceptable dependency." [10] The child's basic orientation to the political system is a supportive one.

More specific orientations to politics that originate in the family have also been uncovered by socialization research. In particular, the structure of paternal orientation is important. The more politicized family begets the more politicized offspring, particularly where both parents' viewpoints are homogeneous and where familial discussion of politics is common.[11] While there may have been continuity in terms of diffuse orientations and possibly party identifications, at least for the period prior to the late 1960s and 1970s, there are now a wide range of specific issues, especially way-of-life and scope-of-governmental action issues that are not shared between the generations. And most importantly, as M. Kent Jennings and Richard G. Niemi document, the gulf between the generations in regard to cynicism has widened between 1965 and 1973.[12] The difference between the generations leads to one inescapable conclusion—that socializing agents other than parents and family are exerting an influence. These other socializing agents in a highly complex and differentiated modern society are the schools and the mass media. In an ideal-type traditional society this would not happen. Instead, generation after generation would be identical. Familial socialization would be all of socialization.

10. David Easton and Jack Dennis, *Children in the Political System* (New York: McGraw-Hill, 1969), p. 137.

11. Richard E. Dawson and Kenneth Prewitt, *Political Socialization* (Boston: Little, Brown, 1969), p. 117.

12. M. Kent Jennings and Richard G. Niemi, "Continuity and Change in Political Orientations: A Longitudinal Study of Two Generations," *American Political Science Review,* 69 (December 1975), 1,331.

Education and the schools represent the greatest challenge to familial socialization. And both of these have a number of components. There are research findings dealing separately with elementary, high school, and college students. There is also a question of whether the presumed effects of education are the results of peer group or curriculum and faculty factors. For example, the famous Bennington study demonstrated the impact of peer groups on attitude conversion of a population of college women in the 1930s.[13] Coming from upper-middle-class and conservative families, they became liberal and favorable to the New Deal program in the Bennington environment. A follow-up study twenty-five years later demonstrated that most of these women maintained their liberalism even outside the Bennington environment in later years. The only departures from this pattern occurred in instances where the respondent's spouse was of a different political persuasion.[14] In both instances it is clear that the immediate peer group—be it one's dormitory mates or marital mates—were very important to the formation and maintenance of attitudes.

The institutional explanation of the effects of education can be viewed as a variant of the peer-group phenomenon. Richard Flacks suggests persuasively that the *concentration* and *segregation* of young people in educational institutions in record numbers in the 1960s account for their special consciousness and political behavior. Flacks writes:

> The rise of mass higher education is one of the most significant and dramatic changes in American society—if for no other

13. Theodore H. Newcomb, *Personality and Social Change: Attitude Formation in a Student Community* (New York: Dryden, 1943).
14. Theodore H. Newcomb, *Persistence and Change: Bennington College and Its Students After Twenty-five Years* (New York: Wiley, 1967).

reason than that it has created "youth" on a mass scale by segregating seventeen to twenty-one year olds in large numbers from other social groups and keeping them from full-time participation in the labor force.[15]

The importance of youth's attention to peer groups is consistent with the argument that in modern society the character of socialization is extrafamilial. This evolution of socialization dynamics has been elaborated in David Riesman's classic, *The Lonely Crowd.*[16] His analysis of emerging socialization by "other direction" dynamics as opposed to "inner direction" ones corresponds to the increased importance of peer groups instead of parents as sources of social and political learning. A major implication of this tendency is that youth, in some sense, becomes a self-fulfilling prophecy. What is incipient among some youth tends to be adopted by increasing numbers of them. This is why the notions of a "youth culture" and a "youth market" have become distinct phenomena in the past few decades.

The tendency toward ever-widening bases for socialization continues beyond the peer group to the mass media of communication and to the values and styles that have become associated with the type of society termed "post-industrial." Again, these stages in the socialization process are analytically distinct only. In reality there is much convergence and interdependence. For example, the realization of the youth market in the 1960s became possible because the media contributed to youth's awareness of itself as a distinct phenomenon.

15. Richard Flacks, *Youth and Social Change* (Chicago: Markham, 1971), p. 36.
16. David Riesman, *The Lonely Crowd* (abridged edition, New Haven: Yale University Press, 1969).

The model of post-industrial society suggests an altered form of social and economic structure and attending values. These values are relevant to the character of political participation. To the extent that these new values shift the political culture, they alter what the individual comes to expect of politics. The model of the post-industrial society describes a basic shift in the social and economic structure of society from one oriented to the production of goods to one oriented to the production of services and their consumption.[17] Necessarily, this new economy is one which depends heavily on advanced educational attainment in order to manage its bureaucracies and new technologies.

This shift in social and economic structure implies a change in public opinion and the attitudinal bases for partisanship as well. Ronald Inglehart has suggested that in societies which are prosperous and which have solved the basic problems of industrial production and the distribution of scarce goods, public opinion, and ultimately the political culture, will turn to new orientations.[18] In particular, the values of self-expression and civil liberties will take precedence over those related to the acquisition of goods and the maintenance of order. Inglehart's findings and interpretation are consistent with a major interpretation of student politics and concerns that appeared in the middle and late sixties. Student protest would appear as a luxury, then, for those who could afford it.

Unfortunately, the validity of these attitudinal implications of the post-industrial model did not survive very far into the

17. Daniel Bell, *The Coming of Post-Industrial Society* (New York: Basic Books, 1973), p. 14.
18. Ronald Inglehart, "The Silent Revolution in Europe: Intergenerational Change in Post-Industrial Societies," *American Political Science Review*, 65 (December 1971), 991–1,017.

1970s. Very rapidly the scarcity of raw-material resources became apparent. Moreover, the specter of unemployment and underemployment came to haunt many of the cadres trained for the new post-industrial needs. A new series of scarcities came to the fore and characterized the human condition much as had the older material and production scarcities previously.

The meaning of post-industrial society is ever-evolving. As a type of society it is in the process of becoming rather than being. Yet, there is apparent a consistent social ethic throughout this evolution in its different stages. Earlier equations of post-industrial society with the affluent society missed the mark. The essential meaning of this type of society is *not* affluence but rather the diminished centrality of industrial production itself as a basis for society. In the new age of natural resource scarcity and attention to ecology, the diminished place of production is as appropriate as the earlier conception of this society which assumed the production needs of society were satisfied and human concern could turn elsewhere. The recent talk of a lowering of material and standard-of-living expectations is consistent with this evolution.

The values associated with post-industrial society could not have had the diffusion and impact that they did were it not for the mass media of communication, particularly television. Sensitivity by the masses to the nonmaterial dimension of the human condition and to the new issues of concern of the sixties —civil rights and the Vietnam war—was possible because of television. According to Daniel Bell, "The introduction of modern mass communication allows us, in many cases forces us, to respond directly and immediately to social issues." [19] Bell goes on to suggest that ". . . the presence of the television

19. Bell, *op. cit.*, p. 315.

cameras in Selma, Alabama, showing the use of crude violence . . . against the black marchers, aroused an immediate national response which was reflected in the presence of thousands of persons who poured into Selma the following week from all over the country." [20]

It is clear that there are two interdependent dimensions to the societal basis of socialization—values and the mass media. The diffusion of new values has been taking place very rapidly and is of consequence to the character of the political culture and the ideational basis of the parties. And television itself both reinforces youth's realization of itself as a distinct social type and makes possible the rapid diffusion of new ideas, styles, and fashions.

The fact of ever-widening bases for socialization points to the possibility of discontinuity in the socialization process. Following the analysis of Dawson and Prewitt, "discontinuity" refers to a situation in which earlier socialization agencies and experiences do not correctly or sufficiently relate to later political learning. It also refers to the situation in which the thrust and substance of the learning from different courses are contradictory.[21] However, the notion of discontinuity has a larger applicability than for the socialization process narrowly construed. Recent socialization dynamics have formed a distinct political generation whose orientation to politics not only is discontinuous with that of older generations but is also inconsistent with the past ideational bases for the political parties.

Political Generations

The argument that recent socialization dynamics have yielded a distinct set of orientations and expectations on the

20. *Ibid.*
21. Dawson and Prewitt, *op. cit.,* p. 81.

part of youth compels attention to the notion of political generations. As elaborated by Karl Mannheim, mere biological contemporaneity, that is, being born in the same period, is not a sufficient indicator of the generation phenomenon as a distinct force in human events. What is required is that the impact of history touch the consciousness of all those in a given age category. The accident of birth at a given time puts one in a "generation location" and nothing more, at least initially. Individuals become an "actual generation" in Mannheim's terms only "insofar as they participate in the characteristic social and intellectual currents of their society and period, and insofar as they have an active or passive experience of the interactions of forces which make up the new situation." [22] The response to these forces by youth need not be uniform or monolithic. Indeed the possibility that segments within the same actual generation can be vastly different is allowed by Mannheim.

> Youth experiencing the same concrete historical problems may be said to be part of the same actual generation; while those groups within the same actual generation which work up the material of their common experiences in different specific ways, constitute separate generation-units.[23]

The existence of generational consciousness, in Mannheim's terms, is very much present because of the impact of television in the mass culture.

Mannheim's distinctions are important to ponder inasmuch as there is nothing in this classic theory of generations that requires the homogeneous or monolithic response of

22. Cited in Philip G. Altbach and Robert S. Laufer (eds.), *The New Pilgrims: Youth Protest in Transition* (New York: David McKay, 1972), p. 119.

23. *Ibid.*, p. 120.

youth in order to merit special attention. Moreover, the aggregate sum of the opinion of youth, such as on the Vietnam war policy, could by itself reveal little of interest. Different segments of youth had different opinions. And it was within distinct segments, such as middle-class versus working-class youth, or college youth versus noncollege youth, that the impact of the civil rights and Vietnam war controversies of the 1960s were clearly registered.

Because these events of the 1960s were sources of strain on the usual party politics, it is not unusual that those least tied to the established parties and party system would respond in divergent ways. There should be no surprise in the observation of Seymour Martin Lipset and Earl Raab that in 1968 George C. Wallace received disproportionate support from the young rather than the old, and within the young, from the less well-educated.[24] And while the net effect of diverging youth segments could yield a result of no difference from the older age categories in the aggregate, it serves, nevertheless, as a telling commentary on the dynamics of change within a generation.

There are two phenomena to be distinguished. The first is an orientation of a given generation at one point in time which is at variance with the orientation of a similar age category at an earlier point. The second phenomenon is change, which characterizes all of society between these points. The clearest expression of this distinction is provided by Jennings and Niemi.[25] In their terms, a generation effect would register a new pattern in a given generation over time, independent of any pattern for the rest of society. A period effect would regis-

24. Seymour Martin Lipset and Earl Raab, *The Politics of Unreason* (New York: Harper & Row, 1970), pp. 392–93.
25. Jennings and Niemi, "Continuity and Change . . ." pp. 1,316–335.

ter comparable change over all generations over time. The first instance refers to the disproportionate impact of history upon the consciousness of a given generation. The second case is one of events effecting a change in the orientations of all generations over time.

Most recent research points to the present predominance of the second model. That is, in most dimensions, change has characterized both the younger and older generations over time. Gerald M. Pomper has demonstrated that on six policy issues both generations have exhibited change in the same direction, presumably due to the nonselective impact of the times. The issues included "federal aid to education, government provision of medical care, government guarantee of full employment, federal enforcement of fair employment and fair housing, federal enforcement of school integration, and foreign aid." [26] Of course, it is an open question whether the changes perceived by Pomper between 1956 and 1968, generally in a more liberal direction, were conditioned by an awareness of what the "acceptable" responses might be as well as by an emerging consensus favoring issues which no longer had the capacity to polarize intensely the population. Similarly, Jennings and Niemi demonstrated intergenerational convergence over several dimensions of behavior and political attitudes. Here, however, there were some exceptions to the pattern due to period effects. Over the period 1965–73, there emerged a greater willingness to perceive differences between the parties on the part of the younger generation, as well as a disproportionately sharp increase in political cynicism.

In yet a third study describing the distribution of opinions

26. Gerald M. Pomper, "From Confusion to Clarity: Issues and American Voters, 1956–1968," *American Political Science Review,* 66 (June 1972), 416–17.

in 1968 over a wide range of concerns, including the Vietnam war, the role of the federal government, civil rights, and political cynicism, the dominant conclusion was that the youth generation was no different from the middle-aged one and that some of the greatest differences were between the old generation—those at least fifty years of age—and everyone else.[27] However, quite correctly, Richard E. Dawson acknowledged that his age categories might be too coarsely drawn, that drawing the line for youth at age thirty could hide the dynamics operative below that threshold. Furthermore, he suggested that:

> The differences between the generations may be more apparent with respect to social norms, behavioral patterns, and morality, rather than on questions of governmental welfare, policies and international involvement.[28]

The following chapter of this essay reveals just how appropriate Dawson's suggestion is.

Youth and a Changing Political Culture

In the most general sense, the political culture, in Gabriel A. Almond's words, refers to "a particular pattern of orientations to political actions." [29] Necessarily, such orientations are present in every political system. In particular, they refer to the accepted modes of citizen participation in the political system, the range of acceptable public policies, and, at the most general level, the very acceptance of the legitimacy of the political system and its processes.

27. Richard E. Dawson, *Public Opinion and Contemporary Disarray* (New York: Harper & Row, 1973).

28. *Ibid.*, p. 129.

29. Cited in Dawson and Prewitt, *op. cit.*, p. 26.

The importance of such orientations is that they are very basic building blocks for the political behavior of individuals and groups, such as races, classes, and age segments. If there is an attenuation of commitment to the political party system, as may be inferred from the declining rate of voting participation and the declining willingness to declare a party identification, the origins of this reduced commitment to the political parties are located very likely in those basic orientations termed the political culture.

Mass political behavior depends upon the character of the political culture. From the perspective of theory, the importance of youth's political patterns lies in their revelation of a changed political culture. Youth then becomes an index to this important attitudinal orientation—the political culture—and to possible shifts in its substantive dimensions. However, while there is agreement on what the political culture is and its importance in the abstract, there are different interpretations on what constitutes the phenomenon in any specific sense. This reflects the different perspectives and priorities of different authors. One's perspective on what is important in politics very much conditions what one will select as the basic components of the political culture.

Of the several items that contribute to the American political culture, two stand out, both because of their fundamental importance to the political system and because of the impact of youth upon them. The first of these is a sense of trust in the political system and its regime. The second is that collection of ideas—in sum an ideational construct—dealing with the place of government in society and the role of the individual. This second system of ideas combines to form the ethos of classical liberalism, which is the basic American political ideology.

In the past the American people have expressed a basic trust in their government and its leaders. This confidence served as a condition for support of the American political system by the citizenry and their contentment with it. Past popular and academic commentary celebrated this basic support by the American people for their government. In particular, past socialization research continually documented the benevolent image of national institutions and leadership, particularly the presidency, held by the youngest persons. Apparently, this age-related differentiation reflected the continuing effect, into early adulthood, of the positive and benevolent images of government inculcated in childhood.

This basic component of the American political culture, political trust, no longer exists as it once did. The major likely reasons for this lack of trust are not difficult to find. Beginning in 1965 an American President directed the escalation of American involvement in the Vietnam war even after winning re-election in 1964 as the temperate, responsible, "peace" candidate. The urban conflagrations of 1967 and 1968 signaled the despair of some in the face of raised expectations for a better life. For others the riots reflected the inability of government to maintain social control. The attending violence contributed directly to the saliency of the "social issue" that dominated the Republican "law and order" campaign themes of 1968 and 1970. And finally there was Watergate and everything implied by it. The American people's realization that their President and top administration leaders committed unlawful acts and then lied about them publicly offered no small contribution to the disillusionment then in process.

Unquestionably, the series of revelations that culminated in the resignation in disgrace by the President affected Americans' confidence in and respect for their government. However, notwithstanding the importance of the Watergate phenomena, it would be a mistake to account for the recent erosion of confidence and support from this basis exclusively. At most, Watergate should be seen as a catalyst for tendencies otherwise in process, tendencies whose bases lie in factors of societal evolution as much as in public events.

There is evidence that disillusionment anteceded Watergate. In the fall of 1973 the Senate Subcommittee on Intergovernmental Relations of the Senate Committee on Government Operations commissioned Louis Harris and Associates, Inc., to survey the public's perceptions of the responsiveness of government.[30] Since Watergate was very much on the public's mind, the survey's findings of a severe loss of confidence by the people in their government is no surprise. However, for the most part, the attitudes expressed in 1973 represented a continuation of trends first noticed in 1966.

Youth reflect emerging currents of opinion. Thus, it is not surprising to discover that as the population as a whole became less trusting and more cynical, the rate of this turn away from trust was greatest for the youngest age cohorts. Jennings and Niemi document this trend in their longitudinal comparison on two age cohorts.[31] The press of political events since 1965 has evaporated the previously existent reservoir of political trust. In addition, the decline in commitment to the political parties is associated with this decline in trust. But antipartyism owes as much to factors of societal evolution as to specific public events. These changes in the parties will be elaborated further in the following chapter.

---

30. United States Senate, Committee on Government Operations, "Confidence and Concern: Citizens View American Government" (Washington, D.C.: U.S. Government Printing Office, 1973).

31. Jennings and Niemi, "Continuity and Change . . ." p. 1,331.

What is impressive about the recent decline in trust and confidence is the rapid diffusion of this sentiment across all segments of the population. Political cynicism, the opposite of political trust, also characterized disappointed conservatives as well as frustrated liberals. Arthur H. Miller has documented that ". . . political cynicism has consistently been most prevalent among those favoring segregation and believing that the federal government should not play a role in the integration of schools and public accommodations." [32] In judging the policies produced by the federal government, both liberals and conservatives have found themselves less trusting and more cynical.

The accelerating turn toward cynicism and its broadening scope in the population led Miller to an interesting insight: that there are cynics of the left and cynics of the right and that these can also be differentiated by demographic characteristics.

One-third of the "cynics of the left" were under 30 whereas only 12 per cent of the most cynical on the right were young. Blacks comprised 38 per cent of the "cynics of the left"; 99.7 per cent of the "cynics of the right" were white. While "cynics of the left" tended to identify more with the Democratic (71 per cent) than the Republican party (12 per cent), those on the right were more evenly split; 48 per cent were Democrats and 35 per cent were Republicans. The "cynics of the right" had higher incomes, with only 21 per cent making less than $4,000 a year; 38 per cent of those on the left were below that figure. *Those on the left, however, were much better educated— 28 per cent had some college training or held a college degree, as compared with only 18 per cent among those of the right. Again, with blacks removed, the percentage of those on the left who had had some college rose to 38 per cent.*[33]

32. Arthur H. Miller, "Political Issues and Trust in Government: 1964–1970," *American Political Science Review,* 68 (September 1974), 951–72.
33. *Ibid.,* p. 962.

Miller demonstrates that the political center is being eroded by both the Left and the Right and that age and education contribute to this emerging polarization. This then constitutes a major way in which age (youth) and education (the educational revolution) contribute to the transformation of American politics. These considerations also highlight an interpretation of recent politics that looks beyond specific public events and includes basic societal factors in the analysis. It can be argued that civil rights, Vietnam, and Watergate had the impact that they did because of the ever-widening scope of socialization dynamics.

The second major component of the political culture is the ethos of classical liberalism. Here, too, the emerging patterns among youth portend an important transformation. Two major principles dominate this ethos—the belief that the impact of government on the lives of the citizenry should be minimal and that each person should advance as far as his initiative and skill will permit. In the idealized world of classical liberalism, *competition,* be it between firms, persons, or political forces, is the dominant method of allocation. In this ultimate test of worth and merit the role of government is merely to "hold the ring," to be an unobtrusive witness to the contention of fortunes and forces. Capitalism and free enterprise are the major institutional expressions of this ethos.

In this view of the world, government is accepted only grudgingly, as a necessary evil to be both endured and controlled. It is small wonder that neither the politician nor the political role has earned much approval. His very craft, government, is suspect. The tenets of the political culture, in its classical liberal and anti-politics expression, have contributed an element of incompatibility with other expressions of the political culture. At the same time that the American citizen inculcated positive support for the major symbols and institutions of the republic, such as the flag and the presidency, he also developed a healthy disrespect for the political persons who functioned in the task of government. Clearly, some degree of cynicism and lack of trust in government was always present.

It is apparent that in recent years and for certain segments of society, the classical liberal basis for American political society has been under indictment. The narrowness of these principles conflicts with the needs posed by an increasingly interdependent and complex society. The writings of Gary Wills, Theodore J. Lowi, and Karl A. Lamb exemplify this trend.[34] Yet, for the majority of the population, the political culture still functions as a secular religion.

The 1972 presidential campaign exemplified the indictment presented by a critical minority and the response of the majority. The message of this Democratic campaign constituted a threat to the dominant bourgeois values of the classical liberal ethos. Because of this, the campaign was doomed to failure. McGovern's proposal for an economic grant to every citizen, posed early in the campaign, violated the dominant ethos of the political culture which stressed competition for achievement. Similarly, the system of quotas for women, Blacks, and youth violated the same norm. Thereafter the lesson for practical presidential politics became very clear. Serious candidates need to avoid proposals and appeals that are incompatible or inconsistent with the basic beliefs most Americans hold. Moreover, the successful candidate will develop an appeal that reflects the underlying beliefs and aspirations of the majority.

34. Garry Wills, *Nixon Agonistes* (New York: New American Library, 1970); Theodore J. Lowi, *The End of Liberalism* (New York: Norton, 1970); and Karl A. Lamb, *As Orange Goes* (New York: Norton, 1974).

The preconvention politics of both Republican and Democratic candidates in 1976 reflected this realization. The contest
between President Gerald Ford and Ronald Reagan for the
Republican presidential nomination proved to be most heated
on foreign policy and defense issues, which do not have the
centrality in the political culture that domestic issues do. On
the Democratic side none of the leading candidates for the
presidential nomination in any sense represented an indictment of the tenets of the political culture. And Jimmy Carter
moved to the front by avoiding any specific issue positions
and instead striking symbolic appeals which resonated well
with the religious character of the mainstream.

Despite the relative absence of any challenge to the political
culture in 1976, the potential for challenge is very much
present. And youth is the source of this challenge. The recognition of youth as a distinct social type produced by common
conditions of socialization implied the phenomenon of a youth
culture. This culture is expressed in terms of orientations and
perspectives that set youth apart from previous generations.
James S. Coleman has characterized youth in terms of a distinct
"inward-lookingness," a psychic attachment of young people
to each other, a press for autonomy from and defiance of older
generations, and a special concern for the underdog.[35] It was
not accidental that a segment of the population that had been
set apart by the rest of society should in turn have viewed itself as a phenomenon apart from the rest.

Two of Coleman's characterizations of the youth culture are
especially relevant to the overall American political culture.
One is the wish for autonomy from and defiance of older generations. The other is concern for the underdog. To the extent

35. James S. Coleman, *et al., Youth: Transition to Adulthood* (Chicago:
University of Chicago Press, 1974), pp. 113–24.

that the "youth movement" has had an existence, it has been
as a phenomenon apart from older age groups. Indeed, one of
the major differences between the recent "New Left" and the
"Old Left" is in the former's rejection of ties to adult organizations. And, as Coleman indicates, support for the underdog
relates directly to the anticompetition and antibusiness ethos
characteristic of the young. "A larger proportion of youth
than of other age groups hold an anticompetitive ethic, because in competition someone must lose, and many youth are
sensitive to this." [36]

Ultimately, the evolving political culture leads to strain on
the party system. No longer operative is an older theory of
party politics that would have the parties stand on the most
common denominator of public opinion, that which is least
controversial to the largest number of supporters or hoped-for
supporters. The former theory of party emphasized competition. This theory's dominant metaphor was the marketplace.
In sum, former American politics emphasized process over
substance, technique over policy. In the market model, policy
outcomes are given. By contrast, the more recent policy
focus begins with the systematic analysis of these choices.
Not coincidentally, the dominant inquiry in American political science until the mid-1960s was consensus; since then, and
increasingly in the 1970s, it is public policy.[37] And this shift
in emphasis from process to substance is itself an indictment
of the classical liberal tenets of the traditional American political culture.

36. *Ibid.*, p. 122.
37. On these points see also Theodore J. Lowi, *The Politics of Disorder*
(New York: Basic Books, 1971), especially the Prologue.

5 | Partisan Decline: Impact of Youth

Virtually every academic and journalistic commentary on recent American political parties notes the decline of party. This study is no exception. Evidence of this partisan decline can be found in the increase of people disassociating themselves by word and deed from the major parties, in reduced rates of voting participation, in the declining correlation of a voter's party identification with his vote for his party's candidate, and the inability of the party system to sustain a constant character of voter response over time. Central to these diverse elements of partisan decline is the present place of party identification. This chapter discusses the recent evolution of party identification and documents the relation of this phenomenon to recent issue positions of the electorate.

Notwithstanding the reduced contribution of party identification to political choice in recent years, this phenomenon is still of value to political analysts. For as an attitude, and as a measure of partisanship independent of political choice in any particular election, the condition of party identification is but another index to the alienation and disengagement of many citizens from the established institutions of government and politics. Furthermore, it is not surprising to discover this lack of commitment to the parties today given the discontinuous character of the socialization process in the modern period. When there is lack of continuity in the political learning of the developing citizen, and when traditional sources of socialization no longer maintain the influence they once did, it would be unrealistic even to expect that partisan commitment would be maintained as before. Although these dynamics are reason enough to expect a decline in partisanship, it is also the case that the inability of the party system to undergo and sustain a new electoral alignment contributes to the gulf between the attitudinal evolution of the population and the character and appeals of the established parties. Rapid attitudinal change is characteristic of the modern mass society. But institutions do not change as rapidly. And parties, as institutions, are inherently antique.

Party Identification
and Generational Theory

Party identification taps the degree of identity of a person to the parties as generalized concepts and points of reference. As researchers have used this variable, individuals have the chance to express themselves as strong Democrats, weak Democrats, Independents, weak Republicans, or strong Republicans. Prior to 1964 the relationship between age and the fact of party identification was not particularly noteworthy. Between 1952 and 1964 the majority of persons in each of the age categories identified themselves as either Democrats or Republicans, as Table 7 reveals, although the percentage of independents was always greater than the percentage of Republicans for voters under thirty-five years old. More specifically, age did not relate appreciably to Democratic identification,

Table 7 | Age by Party Identification

	1952					1956				
	Dem. %	Ind. %	Rep. %	N.	Tot. %	Dem. %	Ind. %	Rep. %	N.	Tot. %
18–24	57.3	24.5	18.2	110	100.0	41.3	39.4	19.2	104	99.9
25–34	50.9	26.7	22.5	405	100.1	45.6	28.6	25.9	406	100.1
35–54	50.2	23.1	26.7	715	100.0	48.1	22.4	29.5	749	100.0
55+	43.7	19.4	37.0	465	100.1	41.1	20.2	38.7	411	100.0
	1960					1964				
18–24	44.4	29.6	25.9	54	99.9	51.9	33.8	14.3	77	100.0
25–34	46.6	27.7	25.7	397	100.0	50.0	28.3	21.7	290	100.0
35–54	47.4	25.6	27.0	844	100.0	53.2	24.4	22.4	635	100.0
55+	44.9	16.8	38.3	572	100.0	52.1	16.4	31.5	505	100.0
	1968					1972				
18–24	36.6	53.5	9.9	101	100.0	35.8	50.9	13.3	391	100.0
25–34	39.2	34.8	25.9	293	99.9	33.4	47.0	19.6	566	100.0
35–54	49.4	27.2	23.3	613	99.9	43.4	33.6	23.0	882	100.0
55+	51.7	18.0	30.3	478	100.0	45.5	21.6	33.0	798	100.1

SOURCE: The election studies of the Center for Political Studies, provided through the Inter-University Consortium for Political Research.

which was strong then in all age categories. By contrast, Republican identification throughout this entire period bore a consistent relationship to age. The younger the age category, the less the Republican strength. A third major observation on age and party identification is the dramatic rise in independent identification in 1968 and 1972. The presence of greater independent identification among the younger voters has been apparent since 1952.[1] However, nothing prior to 1968 anticipated the very sharp increase in independent identification of those aged eighteen to twenty-four, or in the two youngest age segments, those aged eighteen to thirty-four, in 1972.

Two different interpretations of the patterns of age and party identification vie for consideration—life cycle versus generational. Each appraises differently the durability of the changes observed. The life cycle interpretation suggests that younger persons are less firmly fixed both in the habits of political partisanship (more likely to be independent, and if partisan, weak partisans at that) and in the habit of voting itself.[2] They are also more likely to be liberal, although by no means so in all dimensions of public opinion, and become more conservative only later in the life cycle with the responsibilities of family and vocation. From this perspective, any greater liberalism of the young would be attenuated in time as they passed through the life cycle.

Alternatively, the generational interpretation holds that the changes observed, particularly the sharp rise in independent identification, are not consequent to one's position in the life cycle, but are related directly to the stimulus of the experience of public events coming at this early stage of the life cycle,

1. Robert E. Agger, "Independents and Party Identifiers: Characteristics and Behavior in 1952," in Eugene Burdick and Arthur J. Brodbeck, *American Voting Behavior* (New York: The Free Press, 1959), p. 314.
2. Angus Campbell, *et al., The American Voter* (New York: John Wiley & Sons, Inc., 1960), p. 161.

when patterns are not firmly set.[3] The characteristics of a given age group would then be expected to persist when that same group was examined at a later point in time.

Prior to the late 1960s, the life-cycle interpretation dominated expectations for the political behavior of youth. The dominance of this model led to the expectation that any youth vote would be of very little consequence in either the immediate or long run. The only major exception to the life-cycle model was the recognition that the generation that came of age politically during the Great Depression developed a greater Democratic party identification than either the generations preceding or succeeding it.[4] The existence of the New Deal generation in politics is important, as it bears witness to the susceptibility of new generations to the emerging currents of opinion in their time.

There is ample reason to suggest that it is the generational, not the life-cycle interpretation, that accounts for the apartisan behavior of today's youth. The life-cycle interpretation argued that this reluctance to partisan commitment stemmed, in part, from the newness of the young to politics. But this suggestion is uncompelling in this age of ubiquitous television and of heightened political consciousness in response to public events such as the Vietnam war and Watergate. Both the ever-widening bases of socialization, described in the previous chapter, and recent public events have combined to impact disproportionately on the young citizenry. The sharpened skills of the investigative newspaper journalist and the stature of network television news (named by the public as the most credible source of news among all the media) have contrib-

3. In this analysis the independent identification category combines those independent but leaning to Democratic or leaning to Republican as well as those solely independent.
4. Campbell, *op. cit.*, pp. 153–56.

Table 8 | Educational Achievement by Age Category: 1960, 1970

Age and Education Completed	1970	1960
20–24 years		
Less than 4 years high school	19.5%	36.4%
4 years of high school or more	80.5	63.6
1 year of college or more	37.5	23.7
25 years and older		
Less than 4 years high school	44.8	58.9
4 years high school or more	55.2	41.1
1 year college or more	21.2	16.5
4 years college or more	11.0	7.7

SOURCE: U.S. Bureau of the Census, *Current Population Reports,* Series P-20, No. 207, "Educational Attainment: March 1970" (Washington, D.C.: U.S. Government Printing Office, 1970).

uted to the shaping of this age of uncommitment and anti-heroes. Understandably, commitment to the political parties, in terms of a willingness to identify with them, is diminished considerably.

The life-cycle interpretation is also less compelling because of the educational revolution that transpired between 1960 and 1970 and which is continuing only slightly abated.[5] It is the experience of mass higher education that sets this new generation apart from previous new ones. The extent of the education revolution can be appreciated by comparing present educational levels with those of the recent past. Table 8 indicates the degree of change in one decade, between 1960 and 1970. Clearly, among those aged twenty to twenty-four, a

5. The actual benefit to society as well as to the individual's self-satisfaction of this educational revolution is questionable in that the ranks of the highly educated expanded much faster than the capacity of the economy to employ these cadres. Chapter 6 discusses the new meaning of education in this altered opportunity climate.

high school diploma became the norm by 1970, while more than one out of three attended at least one year of college. By contrast, in this age group in 1960, fewer than two of three persons completed high school and fewer than one in four attended college.[6]

The political impact of this demographic change is noteworthy. The college-educated young are disproportionately independent and have been so since the late 1960s. This is the demographic segment that would have been a Republican resource in decades past and is anything but that today. Indeed, it is generational change itself that has disrupted the persistence of the older New Deal model of electoral cleavages in which the better-educated middle class voted Republican and opposed a less well-educated working class that was Democratic.[7] Furthermore, being less committed to the traditional parties, and less likely to develop the habit of consistent partisanship, the new voters are able to respond first to issue concerns rather than to routine party appeals.

In addition to the theoretical expectation of generational behavior there is empirical support for this pattern in recent research of Paul R. Abramson.[8] His secondary analysis of the same surveys analyzed for *The American Voter* and later surveys in the series produced after the 1960 publication of this book show clearly that the generational model is the one that prevails. In this study of age cohorts over the 1952–72 period, there was virtually no increase in strong partisanship in the long run, as the life-cycle model would expect. There

6. Louis M. Seagull, "The Youth Vote and Change in American Politics," *The Annals* (September 1971), p. 91.
7. Paul R. Abramson, *Generational Change in American Politics* (Lexington, Mass.: D. C. Heath, 1975).
8. *Ibid.*, pp. 56–63.

was also no evidence that persons become less independent as they age.

Notwithstanding Abramson's findings and argument, which are in the now-expected direction, a major problem remains. It may be the case that the nonconfirmation of the life-cycle interpretation need not necessarily compel a generational interpretation. For while in gross detail the generational interpretation is appropriate, it will be well to consider, as this study does in the following chapter, whether change perceived in several age segments under the stimulus of events is consistent with the classic theory of political generations.

A major consequence of society's lack of adherence to the life-cycle model of political behavior is overall diminished partisanship. It is also clear that changing patterns of socialization play a large part in these dynamics and are an important key to changing patterns in American politics. Thus, given the impact of specific public events and demographic tendencies, parties have a lesser role in the American polity today. They are less useful to society because they no longer attract the loyalty of voters, especially younger voters. What Richard E. Dawson terms the condition of disarray is entirely appropriate.[9] And it is especially with the noneconomic issues that the parties fail to structure opinion. Dawson's study dealt with the electorate in 1968: ". . . the discrepancy between the concerns of the voters and the positions and concerns articulated by the parties and campaigns in 1968 seem to have been exceptionally great." [10] However, 1968 was not unique in this respect. The declining ability of the party identification groups to structure politics and public opinion across a broad range of

9. Richard E. Dawson, *Public Opinion and Contemporary Disarray* (New York: Harper & Row, 1973).

10. *Ibid.*, p. 9.

issues, and especially for the younger age segments, was evident in 1964 as well as 1972, as will shortly be seen.

Perhaps the major expression of the decline of traditional partisanship is the rise of independent identification, especially by the young and educated. That the young are disproportionately independent in identification is not new. What is different about independent identification today is the sheer amount of this attitudinal trait. More than half of the educated young express it. What is also new is that this sort of independence will not melt into the traditional patterns of partisanship as the young cohort ages, as the life-cycle model of partisanship would expect. These new patterns call into question the model of partisanship that prevailed in the past as well as the differential behavior patterns associated with partisanship and independence.

That there is something radically different about the independent in the period since the late 1960s was voiced by Walter Dean Burnham, who distinguished between "old independents" and "new independents." [11] The old independents correspond to the traditional picture of independents portrayed in *The American Voter*. They are less knowledgeable, less interested, and less participant in electoral politics. The new independents, who demographically are young and college-educated, express behavioral patterns directly opposite from these patterns. The new independents correspond to the active alienated described in chapter 3 and are highly involved in politics or could be mobilized into politics for a given cause or issue. Party itself is not an essential stimulus for their participation.

The distinction between "old independents" and "new in-

11. Walter Dean Burnham, *Critical Elections and the Mainsprings of American Politics* (New York: W. W. Norton & Company, 1970), p. 127.

dependents" and their demographic correlates is evident in the following tables. The 1972 election survey of the Center for Political Studies provided an alternate form of the party identification variable that included "no preference" as well as "independent" as a response category. Thus, it becomes possible to compare new and old independents, with the "no preference" response corresponding to what might be expected of the old independents. Table 9 demonstrates that, for all but

Table 9 | Age by Party Identification: 1972

Age	Dem.	Ind.	No Pref.	Rep.	N.	Tot.
18–24	35.8%	38.1%	12.8%	13.3%	391	100.0%
25–34	33.0	40.3	7.3	19.4	573	100.0
35–54	43.2	29.0	5.0	22.9	887	100.1
55+	44.7	14.5	8.4	32.4	812	100.0

SOURCE: The 1972 election study of the Center for Political Studies, provided through the Inter-University Consortium for Political Research.

the oldest age cohort, the vast proportion of nonpartisan affiliation takes the form of independence instead of no preference. Yet, it must be acknowledged that the greatest concentration of no preference (12.8 per cent) is within the youngest cohort. Very likely this reflects the participation polarization that is found among young people. Some of the demographics of this alternative party identification variable are explored in Tables 10 and 11. As anticipated, there is a positive relationship between education attainment and independence but a negative relationship between educational attainment and voicing no preference.

In Table 11 the relationship between age and party identification controlling on college education is examined. Once again, both independence and no preference are concentrated

Table 10 | Education by Party Identification: 1972

	Dem.	Ind.	No Pref.	Rep.	N.	Tot. %
Elem.	50.1%	14.8%	11.3%	23.8%	533	100.0
High S.	41.1	30.4	7.7	20.8	1364	100.0
College	33.2	33.5	5.2	28.1	184	100.0

SOURCE: The 1972 election study of the Center for Political Studies, provided through the Inter-University Consortium for Political Research.

Table 11 | Age by Party Identification: 1972 (for College-Educated Only)

	Dem.	Ind.	No Pref.	Rep.	N.	Tot.
18–24	38.4%	38.4%	6.3%	17.0%	159	100.1%
25–34	29.2	40.3	7.9	22.7	216	100.1
35–54	33.5	33.5	2.5	30.5	275	100.0
55+	32.3	16.9	4.6	46.2	130	100.0

SOURCE: The 1972 election study of the Center for Political Studies, provided through the Inter-University Consortium for Political Research.

in the youngest age cohorts. However, in the youngest age cohort (as well as in the two oldest ones) controlling on college education diminished by half the no preference response but registered no effect upon the independent response. That is, while 12.8 per cent of all those eighteen to twenty-four expressed no preference (Table 9), only 6.3 per cent of the college-educated in that age group expressed the same response (Table 11). These data reinforce the interpretation that the educational revolution has had a considerable impact on the party system and in the direction away from partisan commitment. Even when there is a choice between declaring independent and no preference, the college-educated young maintain their independent stance.

Partisanship and Policy: 1964–72

In the past, party identification served as a prism through which the individual viewed his political world, especially on the policy issues associated with the New Deal era.[12] Similarly, William H. Flanigan and Nancy H. Zingale assert that ". . . the leading assumption is that partisan identification provides guidance for the public on policy matters—that is, most Americans hold their opinions by following what they perceive to be the view consistent with their partisanship." [13] To the extent that this is the case, public opinion on the major public issues should divide in correspondence to the division on party identification. This expectation is explored below for several different kinds of issues in 1964 and 1968 and to a lesser extent in 1972.

Seven issues posed in 1964 and 1968 have been selected for analysis. Five of these were also present and available for analysis in 1972 data. Each issue has been expressed as a dichotomy, and only persons expressing opinions for or against the issue were included in the computations. Because of this dichotomization, it has been possible to express only one side of each issue controversy in the combined and collapsed Table 12, presenting what is generally accepted as the liberal position. The conservative position is not presented but can easily be determined by subtracting the given percentage from 100 per cent.

The items included reflect three of the most controversial issue clusters in recent decades—the role of the federal government in the economy and the provision of benefits to the

12. Campbell, *op. cit.*, p. 181.
13. William H. Flanigan and Nancy H. Zingale, *Political Behavior of the American Electorate* (third edition, Boston: Allyn and Bacon, Inc., 1975), p. 94.

citizenry, the relations between the races and the role of the federal government in shaping and guaranteeing these relationships, and American involvement in the Vietnam war. While more and other items could tap these dimensions, the issue variables presented here are useful because the same items were posed in two and sometimes three of the years, allowing trend analysis.

The role of the federal government generally and in the economy in particular is reflected in the power, medical care, aid to education, and job or employment items. The employment item presents the distributions by partisanship for those agreeing that "the government in Washington should see to it that every person has a job and a good standard of living." The aid to education item taps support for federal aid for elementary and secondary education. The medical care question probes support for the notion that the federal government ought to help people get doctors and hospital care at low cost. Although the 1972 version of this item is included, it is really a very different question than in 1964 and 1968 because of changes in question content and structure.[14]

The power item taps a general ideological response to the power of the federal government. The dominant conventional liberal response since the New Deal has been to accept a stronger role for the federal government, and accordingly those asserting that the government has not gotten too strong were assigned the liberal pole. Of course, the liberal position

14. In 1972, for the first time, the notion of a government insurance plan was introduced in this question, and respondents were asked to place themselves on a scale ranging from most favorable to a government insurance plan (value 1) to most favorable to a private insurance plan (value 7). Values 1, 2, and 3 were combined as the liberal pole while values 5, 6, and 7 were combined as the conservative response. The mid-point, value 4, was excluded as representing complete indifference.

on the power of the federal government has been in flux, to say the least, since 1972, and this in itself is an interesting and important part of the story of recent changes in opinion and ideology. Whereas the notion of minimal government has been an article of faith with American conservatives for a long time, in recent years some liberals have come to see big government as the enemy too.[15] In any event, these several issues all reflect the controversies of the New Deal electoral alignment, which, in retrospect, may be the last of a series of partisan alignments in American political history.

The data and coefficients in Table 12 all reflect the attenuation of this alignment and the continued partisan disarray. For each of the New Deal items—federal power, medical care, aid to education, and jobs—there is a declining association of partisanship and issue position. Undoubtedly, the decline between 1964 and 1968 reflects the extreme ideological polarization posed by the Johnson-Goldwater presidential contest in 1964. Certainly a relative clarity existed in 1964 regarding what self-assigned Republicans and Democrats professed.[16] The lower liberal support by Republicans on the medical care and job items reflects this ideological polarization.

The most dramatic evidence of alignment attenuation and disarray, however, is in the 1972 data. On the power and medical care items, there is a steep decline in the level of association from 1968 to 1972. As already indicated, the changed content and structure of the medical item may account for that

15. Norman H. Nie with Kristi Andersen, "Mass Belief Systems Revisited: Political Change and Attitude Structure," *The Journal of Politics*, 36 (August 1974), 554.

16. This has been explored extensively and well by Gerald M. Pomper. See "From Confusion to Clarity: Issues and American Voters, 1956–1968," *American Political Science Review*, 66 (June 1972), 415–28.

Table 12 | Partisanship and Issues: 1964, 1968, 1972

	1964	1968	1972	1964	1968	1972
	Federal Power			Medical Care		
Dem.	68.9%	56.4%	41.5%	77.1%	79.5%	57.9%
	(352)	(263)	(149)	(485)	(457)	(226)
Ind.	53.9	37.6	35.0	61.6	61.0	56.7
	(124)	(131)	(113)	(167)	(214)	(177)
Rep.	27.8	25.8	42.9	37.2	44.8	38.4
	(78)	(71)	(90)	(111)	(126)	(91)
Gamma =	.54	.42	.01	.54	.49	.23
	Vietnam War			School Segregation		
Dem.	63.3	62.3	68.6	52.9	54.5	47.6
	(285)	(357)	(641)	(337)	(318)	(423)
Ind.	62.6	60.9	65.1	52.7	40.5	45.6
	(129)	(231)	(529)	(149)	(154)	(350)
Rep.	54.6	66.7	63.8	47.9	38.8	40.5
	(131)	(208)	(340)	(148)	(114)	(205)
Gamma =	.11	−.05	.07	.06	.24	.09
	Rights for Blacks					
Dem.	54.1	55.4	57.4			
	(345)	(321)	(491)			
Ind.	55.0	41.5	55.2			
	(154)	(154)	(401)			
Rep.	32.8	37.8	45.8			
	(97)	(110)	(210)			
Gamma =	.25	.26	.13			
	Aid to Education			Jobs		
Dem.	50.7	48.1		52.0	51.6	
	(307)	(251)		(311)	(284)	
Ind.	42.3	35.0		36.8	30.5	
	(112)	(125)		(91)	(114)	
Rep.	19.4	19.3		24.6	30.1	
	(63)	(57)		(73)	(83)	
Gamma =	.43	.40		.41	.34	

NOTE: The percentages represent those in each partisan category who have an opinion and take the acknowledged liberal side; the numbers beneath each refer to the number of persons represented by the percentage.

SOURCE: The election studies of the Center for Political Studies, provided through the Inter-University Consortium for Political Research.

change. But the power item reflects a fundamental shift in the basis of public opinion in this matter.

Prior to 1972 one of the principal differences between Republicans and Democrats was in the Democrats' advocacy by its leadership and acceptance by its rank and file of a more powerful role for the federal government; the Republicans rejected this belief. The data for 1964 and 1968 attest to the very low Republican acceptance of federal power in general, with only about a quarter of the Republicans not being fearful of it. This pattern is also consistent with a past agenda of politics that emphasized the distribution of economic benefits. Moreover, the liberal thrust on this issue agenda was supported by most of the population, most of whom saw themselves as working-class and had come to accept the tangible benefits of the New Deal program. Indeed, it had been possible for most of the population to support the Republican Eisenhower in the 1952 and 1956 presidential elections because he did not represent a substantial threat to these programs.

The 1964 election, for the first time, did represent a serious challenge to the accustomed role of the federal government and the distribution of economic benefits. In that year the Republican Goldwater attempted to present a clear choice between the parties and presidential candidates and was decisively repudiated by the electorate. What is interesting in the distribution of opinion in that year is the liberalism of the independents, who stand closer to the Democratic partisans than to the Republicans. The opinion of the electorate is responsive to the changing context of candidates and campaigns; the movement of the independents with the opinion of the majority Democrats is an expected one in the context of 1964.

The context of the 1968 election, however, was a vastly different one. In 1964 the challenge to the positive role of the

federal government occurred before there emerged any reason
to doubt this philosophy and approach to government. In
1968 both the urban riots of the previous year and the seemingly interminable Vietnam war gave considerable pause to
the liberal assumption that the national government could
redress problems, both foreign and domestic, if only there was
sufficient power and will. Richard Nixon's election to the
presidency was simply a response to the electorate's lack of
faith in the Democratic programs and assumptions. Not sur-
prisingly, the liberalism of Democrats on the power dimension declined in 1968, and the liberalism of the independents
declined even more. In that year the opinion of the independents was closer to that of the Republicans than to the Democrats. This is to be expected in the context of the 1968 election.
That the opinion of the independents was in the Democratic
direction in 1964 and in the Republican one in 1968 reflects
their lability and their greater similarity to movement rather
than to party phenomena.

The structure of opinion on the issue of federal power
changed greatly in 1972. Democratic support for a stronger
federal government declined, while Republican support for the
same increased. Both groups of partisans finally offered very
similar distributions of opinion regarding federal power. This
yielded a result of no relationship between party identification
and opinion on federal power. This indeed was a novel situation. Undoubtedly, the context of a Republican administration
served to increase Democratic apprehension that the principles
they had long favored were not good in all situations and for
all administrations. Similarly, it is reasonable to expect that
Republicans were more likely to defend federal power under a
national Republican administration than they would have under a Democratic one. Increasingly, therefore, public opinion

has not been favorably disposed toward national governmental power. In the first instance, the Washington-oriented programs and assumptions of New Deal liberalism had lost credibility. Secondly, the very institutions of national politics, the political parties, and the presidency had also lost credibility following the experiences of Watergate and presidential resignation. Moreover, the generalized disenchantment with the national government and its bureaucracy was an important ingredient in President Jimmy Carter's 1976 campaign and election. Suspicion and apprehension of political power is not a novel occurrence in the American political experience, which from the beginning has been concerned with controlling political power. But whether this anti-politics posture is at all sufficient for the needs of society in the post-industrial age is questionable, to say the least.

While the once strong associations between both the economic and power items and partisanship have become attenuated, the comparable associations for the issues in other domains have ranged only from modest to negligible. The Vietnam item taps the distribution of those who disagree with the statement that ". . . we did the right thing in getting into the fighting in Vietnam." While a clear majority opinion was expressed on this issue, party failed to discriminate on this item. Especially in 1968 and 1972, party bore no relationship to this opinion, which was supported similarly by all party segments.

The school segregation and Black rights items tap the race issue, which together with Vietnam dominated the public's political consciousness in the middle and late 1960s. The school segregation item presents the distribution of those agreeing that "the government in Washington should see to it that white and Negro children go to the same schools." The

Black rights item presents the distributions of those asserting that the federal government ought to see to it that Blacks get fair treatment in jobs. In general, these data exhibit the greater cleavage among Democrats, who are split in roughly equal measure between the liberal and conservative divisions, and the greater homogeneity of the Republicans, who are more conservative on these items. The more heterogeneous character of Democratic opinion and the more homogeneous character of Republican opinion is consistent with the evolution of the parties since the New Deal.

Given the evidence of modest and declining relationships between party identification and opinion, it is necessary to explore the extent to which age contributes to these patterns. It is a reasonable expectation that youth is less committed to orthodox opinions of past decades and more susceptible to emerging currents of opinion. Indeed, the phenomenon of generational replacement is one reason why past electoral alignments have been bounded in time.

Table 13 presents the distribution of opinion by age categories. Contrary to reasonable expectations, virtually all research suggests that age makes little difference across most, but not all, issues. Indeed, if anything, it is the oldest age group whose opinions stand apart from those of the rest of the population.[17] This was especially the case on the Vietnam issue, which consistently revealed an inverse relationship between age and support for American involvement in the war.[18] Indeed, one of the most provocative of recent findings in public opinion is that youth, in the aggregate, dispropor-

17. On this point see Dawson, *op. cit.,* pp. 124–25.
18. In addition to Dawson, see also John E. Mueller, *War, Presidents and Public Opinion* (New York: John Wiley & Sons, Inc., 1973) and Milton J. Rosenberg, Sidney Verba, and Philip E. Converse, *Vietnam and the Silent Majority* (New York: Harper & Row, 1970).

Table 13 | Age and Issues: 1964, 1968, 1972

	1964	1968	1972	1964	1968	1972
	Federal Power			Medical Care		
18–24	61.5%	46.8%	37.7%	70.5%	64.5%	56.6%
	(32)	(37)	(52)	(43)	(55)	(73)
25–34	60.5	41.0	38.6	61.1	60.1	48.5
	(115)	(86)	(76)	(135)	(137)	(99)
35–54	52.2	44.3	37.8	61.5	65.3	49.0
	(223)	(205)	(110)	(308)	(323)	(169)
55 +	51.9	40.9	42.8	66.3	70.9	59.6
	(181)	(141)	(116)	(272)	(292)	(159)
Gamma =	.10	.03	–.06	–.04	–.13	–.07
	Vietnam War			School Segregation		
18–24	29.5	54.6	59.7	51.6	55.8	57.0
	(13)	(53)	(213)	(33)	(53)	(188)
25–34	29.9	56.4	59.2	56.5	51.0	45.6
	(58)	(150)	(299)	(135)	(150)	(299)
35–54	35.5	58.2	65.0	53.6	47.9	41.6
	(136)	(301)	(495)	(278)	(257)	(293)
55 +	52.6	75.8	77.1	46.3	39.5	42.8
	(142)	(300)	(521)	(186)	(153)	(281)
Gamma =	–.29	–.26	–.23	.11	.16	.12
	Rights for Blacks					
18–24	51.7	52.7	62.3			
	(31)	(49)	(205)			
25–34	51.5	52.8	54.2			
	(122)	(131)	(244)			
35–54	50.0	46.4	51.9			
	(257)	(246)	(349)			
	46.8	43.4	51.7			
	(188)	(168)	(313)			
Gamma =	.06	.11	.09			
	Aid to Education			Jobs		
18–24	53.3	45.5		58.3	43.5	
	(32)	(35)		(28)	(40)	
25–34	44.4	38.0		40.1	44.9	
	(95)	(87)		(87)	(105)	
35–54	39.3	39.2		40.9	39.9	
	(205)	(200)		(201)	(203)	
55 +	36.2	31.0		41.8	36.5	
	(144)	(116)		(161)	(139)	
Gamma =	.12	.12		.02	.10	

NOTE: The percentages represent those in each age category who have an opinion and take the acknowledged liberal side; the raw N.'s for each percentage are placed directly below each percentage.

SOURCE: The election studies of the Center for Political Studies, provided through the Inter-University Consortium for Political Research.

tionately supported the war as compared to older, especially the oldest, segment of the electorate. For example, in 1964 the oldest segment was about equally split on Vietnam involvement as compared to the youngest two age categories, in which supporters of involvement were more than twice as numerous as opponents. Indeed, in all but the oldest age segment, a substantial majority supported involvement. By 1968 all age categories opposed involvement, but again, except for the oldest age segment, this opposition was barely a majority one. The same tendency was expressed in 1972.

This surprising support for war by the young and educated was in fact anticipated in earlier research. Putney Snell and Russell Middleton were early discoverers of the more ready support for war by college men.[19] Given the popular association between youth and the antiwar movement, it is surely ironic that, in the aggregate, it was the oldest, not the youngest, who were proportionately more disposed against involvement in the war.

Despite the Vietnam war opinion distributions of youth in the aggregate, it is well to recognize that opposition to the war was centered among the young, particularly Jewish youth, at the better universities.[20] This stands as an important qualification and elaboration of the finding that opposition to the war by youth was located disproportionately within the "better" colleges and universities. As John E. Mueller suggests, it is insufficient and misleading to link the presumed liberalism associated with the better colleges to the antiwar opinion, inasmuch as the better universities have also been bastions of conservatism. Rather, it is the general liberalism of Jews and their

19. Putney Snell and Russell Middleton, "Student Acceptance or Rejection of War," *American Sociological Review,* 27 (October 1962), 655–67.

20. Mueller, *op. cit.,* p. 141.

concentration in the better colleges and universities that has had an important impact on opinion there.[21] The dimensions of liberalism by Jews in academia as well as their disproportionate anti-Vietnam war stance have been documented again in the important study of the academic community by Everett Carll Ladd, Jr., and Seymour Martin Lipset.[22]

Not only does the impact of age on the issue of war involvement differ from what is popularly believed, but the impact of age on the other opinion items generally has not been very sharp. Yet, it is noteworthy that, for the economic items, the youngest age segment demonstrated greater lability. Over the course of two and three points in time, the oldest age segment was considerably more stable, as could be expected. Thus, it can be argued that evidence is emerging which suggests that age does relate to the attenuation of the New Deal in the opinions of the public. It is not at all surprising that, in the 1976 Democratic presidential primaries and public opinion polls, the candidates most closely associated with the New Deal inheritance (Senators Jackson and Humphrey) were supported more heavily by older age segments. Thus, with the decline of the older economic class basis of the parties, the opportunity emerges for divisions on other kinds of issues or, alternatively, the emergence of a party politics unrelated to opinion cleavages in the electorate.

Decline of the New Deal Alignment

Further evidence that youth is contributing to the attenuation of the New Deal alignment lies in the absence of a rela-

---

21. *Ibid.,* pp. 165–66.
22. Everett Carll Ladd, Jr., and Seymour Martin Lipset, *The Divided Academy: Professors and Politics* (New York: McGraw-Hill, 1975), pp. 158–60.

tionship between class and party identification on the part of
the younger segments of the population. Table 14, controlling
on age level, reveals the association of subjective class identification with partisanship. Indeed, in 1972, among those aged
eighteen to twenty-four the party identification distributions
were virtually constant across the classes. By contrast, in the
two oldest age segments the working class was more Democratic while the middle class was disproportionately Republican, as would have been expected in the era of the New Deal
alignment.

Table 14 | Class by Party Identification by Age: 1972

	Dem.	Ind.	Rep.	N.	Tot.	
18–24						
	%	%	%		%	
Working Class	35.1	49.8	15.2	211	100.1	
Middle Class	36.9	52.5	10.6	179	100.0	Gamma = −.08
25–34						
Working Class	35.1	48.3	16.6	296	100.0	
Middle Class	30.4	48.1	21.5	270	100.0	Gamma = .11
35–54						
Working Class	51.2	32.7	16.1	465	100.0	
Middle Class	34.8	34.8	30.5	400	100.1	Gamma = .32
55 +						
Working Class	49.7	21.8	28.5	459	100.0	
Middle Class	36.7	25.1	38.2	327	100.0	Gamma = .22

SOURCE: The election studies of the Center for Political Studies, provided
through the Inter-University Consortium for Political Research.

The attenuation of the New Deal alignment in American
politics is a response to the unconcern of many in the newer
generations with the sorts of things that seemed important to

and were identified with party ideology to their parents. It reflects the emergence of political conflict on noneconomic matters. These new concerns include those of race, life-style, status conflict, and the character of political engagement. In sum they point to an altered style of political and social life. The 1972 data of the Center for Political Studies provides, for the first time, some newer opinion items that are structured better by age than are the older ones. Table 15 demonstrates these new strong associations. The items chosen deal with women's rights, public protests, and acting outside the law when one feels the cause is just.

The women's rights, or liberation, item presents the distribution of opinions favoring an equal role for women in running business, industry, and government, as opposed to asserting that women's place is in the home. A majority in each category agreed with the women's liberation position, which is taken as the liberal position, but there was a clear relationship of age with support for the liberal position here. The younger the age category, the more substantial was the majority for women's rights.

Similarly, on the protest item the impact of age is clear. Although more than twice as many persons disapprove than approve (68 per cent) of taking part in protest meetings or marches, even though they may be permitted by the local authorities, only in the youngest age category is there majority sentiment for this action. The same distribution of opinion prevails regarding approval of someone who would go to jail rather than obey a law felt to be unjust. Finally, although an overwhelming majority (88 per cent) disapproved of obstructing the government with mass action, this disapproval was strongly related to age—the older the age category, the greater the degree of disapproval.

It is obvious that these are the sorts of concerns for which

Table 15 | Age by New Issues: 1972

	Pro	Con	N.	Tot.	
	Women's Rights *				
18–24	72.5%	27.5%	313	100.0%	
25–34	63.2	36.8	454	100.0	
35–54	59.9	40.1	659	100.0	
55 +	55.8	44.2	584	100.0	Gamma = .16
	Sit-in **				
18–24	23.9	76.1	222	100.0	
25–34	14.3	85.7	363	100.0	
35–54	11.7	88.3	596	100.0	
55 +	5.8	94.2	555	100.0	Gamma = .37
	Law Refusal **				
18–24	51.4	48.6	210	100.0	
25–34	33.9	66.1	316	100.0	
35–54	26.6	73.4	548	100.0	
55 +	14.5	85.5	511	100.0	Gamma = .42
	Protest Approval **				
18–24	63.1	36.9	187	100.0	
25–34	47.5	52.5	295	100.0	
35–54	29.4	70.6	534	100.0	
55 +	14.6	85.4	541	100.0	Gamma = .54

* The recodes here collapsed a seven-point scale of preference into a dichotomy. The midpoint of the scale was excluded as were expressions of "no opinion." The polar opposites of the scale were (1) women and men should have an equal role versus (2) women's place is in the home.

** The recodes here exclude the intermediate category of "depends, pro-con" as well as expressions of nonopinion. Throughout, only clear expressions for or against were used.

SOURCE: The election studies of the Center for Political Studies, provided through the Inter-University Consortium for Political Research.

age matters. But to what extent do the parties structure these concerns? Table 16 explores this avenue. In the case of 1972 evidence, it is apparent that, in general, party fails to structure these opinions in a decisive fashion. That is, where there is substantial approval for a position, such as for women's rights, it is across all party categories. Conversely, where there is massive disapproval, as for the obstruction of the activity of government, it is expressed by all three partisan categories, although there is considerably more support for this position among Democrats and independents than among Republicans. What is most interesting here, however, is the closer cleavage within the Democratic ranks as compared to the Republican in regard to the three items dealing with political action. In terms of opinion about the style of political action, there is no doubt that Republican opinion is virtually monolithic in its disapproval of nonroutine political participation. And given the relationship between age and these new opinion items in 1972, there is reason to expect that the greater polarization within the Democratic side will increase rather than diminish. This is likely inasmuch as young voters are thinking of themselves as Democrats or independents, but not as Republicans. Further evidence for this possibility of increased intraparty polarization is seen in Table 17. It is quite clear that it is in such disproportionate partisanship on the part of the young that youth will have a great impact on American politics. The infusion of youth into Democratic and independent attachments, but not Republican ones, can not help but contribute to an altered tone of political discourse and political conflict.

As expected, the association of party and opinion on the new items tends to be stronger in the two youngest age categories. The only noteworthy exception is in the support of protest meetings and marches, which characterizes a majority

Table 16 | Partisanship by the New Issues: 1972

	Pro	Con	N.	Tot.	
	Women's Rights				
Dem.	60.3%	39.7%	811	100.0%	
Ind.	65.5	34.5	721	100.0	
Rep.	57.4	42.6	465	100.0	Gamma = .01
	Sit-in				
Dem.	13.6	86.4	683	100.0	
Ind.	14.8	85.2	593	100.0	
Rep.	5.6	94.2	446	100.0	Gamma = .22
	Law Refusal				
Dem.	25.7	74.3	634	100.0	
Ind.	37.0	63.0	541	100.0	
Rep.	15.6	84.4	392	100.0	Gamma = .10
	Protest Approval				
Dem.	32.1	67.9	639	100.0	
Ind.	40.9	59.1	499	100.0	
Rep.	19.4	80.6	402	100.0	Gamma = .14

SOURCE: The election studies of the Center for Political Studies, provided through the Inter-University Consortium for Political Research.

of all young people—be they Democrats, independents, or Republicans. On this item there is a clear generational split for the Democrats, with a substantial majority of those under age thirty-five facing an even greater majority over age thirty-five who oppose nonroutine political behavior. Apparently, Republican championing of the "silent majority" was consistent with the opinion bases of the party groups and the opportunities they presented.

These tendencies will make it more difficult for the American party system, specifically the two-party system, to undergo a traditional regeneration or realignment. Opinions on the items of Table 17 reflect a politicization not on the substance of governmental programs but on the character and style of

Table 17 | Partisanship by the New Issues, Controlling on Age: 1972

	18–24	25–34	35–54	55 +	18–24	25–34	35–54	55 +
	Women's Rights				Protest			
	%	%	%	%	%	%	%	%
Dem.	74.8	63.7	58.8	53.9	65.1	58.6	30.6	15.4
	(83)	(93)	(167)	(139)	(41)	(51)	(74)	(37)
Ind.	74.5	65.1	63.6	57.7	63.9	51.1	33.3	18.9
	(120)	(138)	(138)	(75)	(62)	(68)	(54)	(20)
Rep.	59.5	58.4	57.2	56.5	59.1	26.9	22.2	10.3
	(22)	(52)	(87)	(105)	(13)	(18)	(28)	(19)
Gamma =	.14	.05	.00	–.04	.06	.36	.10	.14
	Law Refusal				Sit-in			
Dem.	50.8	35.6	27.0	12.3	30.4	16.5	13.7	6.1
	(32)	(36)	(66)	(27)	(24)	(18)	(36)	(14)
Ind.	55.7	43.0	30.5	20.4	23.1	17.5	13.3	6.6
	(64)	(61)	(53)	(22)	(25)	(29)	(26)	(˙8)
Rep.	29.6	12.3	19.0	12.2	12.5	3.8	5.9	5.1
	(8)	(8)	(24)	(21)	(4)	(3)	(8)	(10)
Gamma =	.13	.24	.10	–.02	.27	.28	.22	.07

NOTE: The percentages represent those in each age and party category favoring the issue. The numbers in parentheses beneath each percentage are the numbers of persons represented by each particular percentage.

SOURCE: The election studies of the Center for Political Studies, provided through the Inter-University Consortium for Political Research.

political action. Taken to its logical conclusion, this ultimately represents a denial of a politics concerned with policy and program. Moreover, these new items of politics, because they are tinged with moralism, are not resolvable in the manner in which the older economic items were.

The past theory of party in American politics celebrated consensus on institutions and procedures as a foundation for manageable conflict on policy. The emerging character of an American electorate with no such consensus suggests the difficulty of emphasizing a policy-oriented politics. And the policy approach becomes even more difficult and problematic when the policies turn on life-styles, morality, and living up to the promised, but less feasible, American dream. How ironic that the very demographic changes that have precipitated a more policy-conscious politics are also the ones that make more difficult a political process premised on solving these concerns.

6 | New Aspects of Politics

Some five decades ago Charles E. Merriam heralded the behavioral revolution in political science with the publication of a volume of essays which expressed observations that seem contemporary in character.[1] Merriam wrote of ". . . coming into a new world, with new social conditions and with new modes of thought and inquiry."[2] He wrote that ". . . the spread of education is a fundamental feature in the construction of a new attitude toward government."[3] He continued that ". . . the whole basis of political reasoning is rapidly being altered by general education."[4] Moreover, he suggested that

1. Charles E. Merriam, *New Aspects of Politics* (third edition, University of Chicago Press, 1970), originally published in 1925.
2. *Ibid.*, p. 85.
3. *Ibid.*, p. 87.
4. *Ibid.*, p. 88.

". . . politics must reckon with a new world which in time and space are fundamentally altered; a new world of universal leisure; a new world of universal education; a non-traditional state of mind; a world of scientific methods and results; a race of beings master of nature's forces in greater measure than before dreamed possible; the participation of the bulk of the community in its fundamental conclusions." [5] Expectations and observations such as these came to represent the behavioral revolution in political science. But what is new in political science today is the very inadequacy of some of the theories and expectations of Merriam, his students, and his students' students. Increasingly, the vocabulary of political analysis and the reality of political events may not be matched very well. Our ability to gauge political phenomena has been compromised by the very persistence of theories and understandings that may no longer be appropriate. In particular, the dichotomy between "life-cycle" and "generational" interpretations of aging and partisanship, the meaning and role of education in the contemporary society and polity, and the very theory and language of realignment may need review.

Political and Party Change

Recent political change seems to follow a course unanticipated by our theoretical inheritance. Since 1964 the image of American parties and politics has changed fundamentally. Prior to that time, the image of a stable two-party system sustained by and contributing to political consensus was conventionally accepted. Since that time great changes have taken place, especially in presidential balloting. Routine stability, measured either in terms of the social bases of the vote or in the electoral outcome, is no longer the norm. The two-party

5. *Ibid.*, p. 101.

system has been challenged by a serious third-party movement in 1968 and is still challenged by the greater threat of apathy and unconcern. Fewer and fewer citizens care to identify with the conventional parties. Consensus regarding basic social values and the legitimacy of political institutions no longer prevails.

The purpose of these chapters on youth in American politics has been to probe and place in perspective these changes. This study does *not* suggest that youth caused these changes, for surely what is new in American politics and the party system might have happened anyway, if not quite as soon. The analysis and argument do suggest, however, that youth has contributed disproportionately to these tendencies, which are registered more clearly among the young. At the same time, the focus on youth allows, indeed encourages, a consideration of these larger contexts and problems. The study of American politics profits, thereby, from the use of micro and macro perspectives. The behavior of youth exemplifies the former; the evolution of values and institutions reflects the latter.

Three changes in particular have been affected by, and are illuminated by, the patterns of youth. They are: the decline of the New Deal alignment; the decline of partisanship, particularly party identification as a cueing device in the electorate; and the rise of "event" and "issue" politics. All three changes reflect the less durable character of the established parties. However, the changes do not suggest any diminution of politics as a concern of the citizenry, but merely the possibility of its expression in different modes.

The decline of the New Deal alignment is reflected in the declining relationship of both subjective social class and the older economic issues with partisanship. Again, these tendencies are clearest for the young. And in place of these older concerns is increasing attention to those of life-style and the legitimacy of new styles of political action. These concerns are intrinsically less capable of being accommodated by compromise. This accounts for the polarization in the Democratic party in 1972 between "old guard" labor and economic liberals versus the moralist young amateurs. In the 1976 Democratic presidential primaries the same polarization was apparent in terms of the different constituencies of Senator Henry Jackson and Representative Morris Udall, with Udall being supported disproportionately by the young, the affluent, and the educated.

The inability of the political process to create and sustain a new alignment is a fundamental departure from previous experience, in which alignment era followed alignment era. Furthermore, the kind of mechanism leading away from alignment, societal change, is precisely the sort of basis that sustained the existence of previous alignments. The change in the population in the decade previous to the New Deal, the rise of an immigrant laboring class in the northern cities, was one of the bases of realignment precipitated by the 1932 election. It was a matter of social evolution leading to political change. By contrast, social and population change today are not leading toward partisan commitment and alignment, but away from such commitment and attachment.

The antipartisan impact of societal evolution has been discussed forcefully by Walter Dean Burnham, who argues that the American electorate is being realigned today but in a direction that will culminate in the end of the traditional two-party system and the tradition of durable alignments.[6] Essentially,

6. Walter Dean Burnham, "American Politics in the 1970's: Beyond Party?" in William Nisbet Chambers and Walter Dean Burnham (eds.), *The American Party Systems* (second edition, New York: Oxford University Press, 1975), pp. 308–57.

this is the result of the emergence of a series of issues in 1964, 1968, and 1972 on which polarization was unrelated to partisan attachment at the same time as there was no increase in partisan attachment. On balance, the polarization on these issues in the mass electorate should have contributed to Republican commitment, but they did not. And this transformation of the mass electorate was accelerated by the patterns of youth on these new issues. Thus, not only is the New Deal electoral alignment in decline, but there are no signs of its replacement by an alternative alignment.

The second major change to which youth contributed is the declining capacity of party to structure opinion, to provide cues by which voters could align on issues, especially on the newer issues. Of course, this particular change follows from the first. Electoral realignment represents both a durable shift in the social basis of the vote and usually a predictable stance by the partisans on a broad and integrated range of public opinion items. In times of alignment decline and nonreplacement the existence of a lesser relationship between party and opinion is plausible. Here again, it is for the youngest age groups that party has the least consequence for opinion stance.

This second change is consistent with the diminished place of party in society. The evidence of declining rates of voting participation, increased cynicism about parties and politics, and instability in electoral outcomes all point to a less secure and a reduced place for party in society. In an older perspective on political behavior, analysts began with demographic (place of residence) and sociological (class, religion, race) variables and predicted to partisanship.[7] A more recent

7. Paul Lazarsfeld, *et al.*, *The People's Choice* (New York: Columbia University Press, 1944).

emphasis began with partisanship as a given response to socialization dynamics and related this partisanship to issues
and voting behavior.[8] In the language of social research,
party, in the first instance, was a dependent variable while
in the second instance an independent one. But, increasingly,
partisanship is best seen as neither of these, at least in any
consistent sense.

In the absence of a firm basis for, or position for, party in
the society, its utility for and use by the electorate will be
variable. It is a resource, then, to be used on occasion. Gerald
M. Pomper's characterization of the voter as a "responsive"
rather than "dependent" creature is apt.[9] This increased responsiveness to events can take place without parties at all, or
at least without parties as institutionalized activity patterns
and tendencies.

The new emphasis on issue awareness as a basis for political choice, which is the third major dimension of the new party
system, corresponds to the rise of "event" as opposed to
"process" politics.[10] As elaborated by Sidney Hyman, this
distinction between event politics and process politics has implications for political participation generally and electoral
participation specifically. Hyman's analysis dealt with student
involvement in the 1970 elections. Even so, he touched a
theme reflective of new political patterns generally. Increasingly, the party system is buffeted by those aroused by an
event, a cause, or an issue, but lacks an enduring commitment by these same persons to the routine of electoral
politics.

8. Angus Campbell, *et al., The American Voter* (New York: John
Wiley & Sons, Inc., 1960).

9. Gerald M. Pomper, *Voters' Choice* (New York: Dodd, Mead, 1975).

10. Sidney Hyman, *Youth in Politics* (New York: Basic Books, 1972),
pp. 17–18.

What is missing in the selective and intense commitment of young political activists is the sense of compromise which made viable the older two-party system. And again, these alternative types of partisans are exemplified by the process of Democratic presidential primary politics in the spring of 1976. The ill-fated candidacy of former Senator Fred Harris was championed by a small group of activists who could not move comfortably over to another candidate, say Representative Morris Udall, who otherwise was ideologically close to Harris. There was little exchange value to the currency of support for Harris or Udall. By contrast, Senator Henry Jackson was supported by many who otherwise would have voted for Senator Hubert Humphrey. A sense of compromise motivated the latter group of voters, who also were older and accustomed to the formerly dominant model of stable two-party competition.

The political action represented by the new activists is akin to, although not the same as, that of the "amateur" politician elaborated by James Q. Wilson. For the amateur type had more in common with process than event politics. His commitment and point of view were generalized to several issues and campaigns. Often it was institutionalized in reform club politics.[11] The demographics, youth and high educational attainment, are the same for both, but the ability to sustain involvement over time differentiates the two types. Indeed, the McGovern supporters of 1972 were notably absent in Democratic presidential nominating politics in 1976. This is not to disparage the occasional role of activists and amateurs in politics, especially in presidential nomination politics. They dominated the Republican national convention in 1964 and the Democratic one in 1972; they were a major force at the

11. James Q. Wilson, *The Amateur Democrat* (Chicago: University of Chicago Press, 1962), pp. 3–5 and *passim*.

Democratic convention in 1968. It is merely to assert that such involvement is unpredictable.

There is a consistent and integrated character to recent political evolution. The decline in the last great alignment and the unlikelihood of its replacement relates to the reduced role of party in society and the declining capacity of parties to serve as strong cue-giving phenomena. It is no wonder, then, that youth's involvement in politics has been a highly selective and cause-oriented one.

The inability to create and sustain a new alignment is a serious but not fatal problem for the polity. The failure of realignment is indicative of the passing of an older style of political action. Such a development is serious in that it reflects a turning away from politics at the very time that the need for politics and government is of great importance.

The need for government is an increasing rather than a lessening one, and for two principal reasons. The first is the increased scope of representation in modern American politics. Previously, minorities were quiescent; now they are articulating their claims forcefully. The negotiating skills of the politician and the integrating contributions of institutions such as broad and coalitional parties are called for in a most serious way.

The second reason for an increased need for government lies in the interdependent and complex character of post-industrial society. As Daniel Bell declares, "The post-industrial society . . . requires increasing amounts of coordination, especially when that game is carried on in a visible political arena rather than through the 'invisible hand' of the economic marketplace." [12] Organization, planning, regulation, and government are called for as never before. In post-industrial society,

12. Daniel Bell, *The Coming of Post-Industrial Society* (New York: Basic Books, 1973), pp. 468–69.

the viability of the antigovernment ethos as an organizing principle for the political system is stretched beyond redemption. Thus, the antipolitics and antigovernment rhetoric fashionable today ill serves the needs of society. There is need for planning and management in the political sphere as much as in the private one.

Accounting for Political Change

The benefits of an integrated and contextual approach to American politics lie not only in the characterization of a phenomenon but in its explanation as well. In particular, changes in American party politics can be seen as tendencies that would have occurred irrespective of the Vietnam war and Watergate. Of course these events contributed to the tendencies in process, especially for the younger segment of the population. But attention to the larger picture of American politics and to the societal conditions for political action helps in avoiding the trap of placing too much emphasis on the immediate and proximate conditions at the expense of underlying ones.

In the largest sense, one general condition underpins emerging political tendencies: modern society. Of course it is in the refinement of this notion and in its specific application that its best use will emerge. The process of individual maturation in modern society leads to personal independence. However, increasingly, the condition of youth has been one of dependence. One of the paradoxes of growing up in modern American society is the individual's prolonged dependence on his nuclear family at the same time as he is searching to assert his independence. The same condition prevails in the experience of secondary and higher education.

Modern societies invest heavily in education. In particular, American society has sustained this investment with the ethos of status by achievement and equality of opportunity. Commitment to this investment reached its peak in the 1960s, and this led to the concentration and segregation of youth, which was a factor in the youth culture and movement. But whatever inconvenience or frustration attended the education experience for youth, there was very little questioning of the ultimate practicality of the college degree. True enough, the counterculture was predicated upon a repudiation of the practical career or vocation and the routes to it. For others, the seeming affluence of the times did not compel a need to take vocation and career that seriously. But no one then doubted that education could lead to the good and material life existence if one wanted it to. By the mid-1970s this has changed in a fundamental way, leading to a possibly radical change in the meaning of education for political analysis.

Previously, education was associated with "positive" outcomes for the political system. An intelligent, well-educated electorate was seen as an important condition for responsible popular government. Education then was viewed as beneficial to the person and to the political system. Philip E. Converse summed up, and, indeed, espoused, this orthodox perspective:

> Whether one is dealing with cognitive matters such as levels of factual information about politics . . . or such motivational matters as degree of attention paid to politics . . . or questions of actual behavior, such as engagement in any of a variety of political activities from party work to vote turnout itself; education is everywhere the universal solvent, and the relationship is always in the same direction. The higher the education, the greater the good values of the variable.[13]

13. Philip E. Converse, "Change in the American Electorate," in *The Human Meaning of Social Change*, Angus Campbell and Philip E. Converse (eds.) (New York: Russell Sage Foundation, 1972), p. 324.

Very likely, the element in education's "positive" effects was the sense of personal efficacy that led to political efficacy. Undoubtedly, a sense of advantage and the reality of opportunity that followed educational attainment led to the condition of confidence and efficacy. All of this was possible because of an adequate match between market opportunities and personal expectations. Such is less the case today.

It is now apparent that the commitment to education exceeded the capacity of the economy to absorb these highly educated new cadres. The U.S. Bureau of Labor Statistics indicates that by the mid-1980s there will be 800,000 more college graduates in the labor force than job openings for them. This results in underemployment, of being forced to accept jobs below one's level of training and expectation.[14]

The political implications of this reversal are profound and consistent with the emerging tendencies in American politics. The new generation is less trusting and supportive and more cynical. Theirs is an alienation due only in part to public events and surely, to some degree, to personal frustration as well. From the perspective of these young persons, more than just the parties lack sense and credibility. The major institutions, beliefs, purposes, and their position in society are open to question as well. For it is a profoundly different matter to turn away from achievement and materialism when there is a choice to be had, as in the case of the counterculture of the 1960s, than when it is compelled by necessity.

Individualism and the valuation of education are important dimensions of modern society. From a sociological perspective, modernity is expressed in terms of the mass society popu-

14. Robert Roth, "Highly-Trained College Grads are Filling Low-Skill Jobs," *The Philadelphia Bulletin*, July 17, 1975, p. 11. See also, James O'Toole, "The Reserve Army of the Underemployed," *Change*, May 1975.

lated by atomized individuals. From a historical perspective, modernity is expressed in terms of the post-industrial society which emphasizes educational attainment. The imperatives of both types of society reinforce each other. Individualism is feasible only in an egalitarian society. Educational attainment becomes an important basis of differentiation and competition in such a society. In other respects as well the characteristics of the mass and post-industrial societies offer mutual support and convergence. Both types emphasize the mass media, large-scale bureaucratic organization, service economies, and egalitarianism. Technology made possible both the post-industrial society and the mass media. In turn, relative societal affluence contributed to the imperative toward equality. So different is contemporary society from that which existed previously that it is no wonder that the relatively antique institution of the American party system is in difficulty.

From Party to Movement

While commitment to routine party politics will wane, especially for young people, interest in politics, even electoral politics, could remain high. The model of voting presented in *The American Voter* equated interest and commitment to politics with commitment to party politics.[15] But this equation need not hold, given the impact of education on political participation. For some, the expression of this interest will take the form of movement action. Thus, the changed character of the party system suggests the increased importance of social and political movements as mechanisms of collective action. This impact will be felt especially on the presidential nomination process. This is a far cry from asserting that the parties themselves will become more like movements. The latter imply a

15. Campbell, *op. cit.*, p. 111.

concentration of collective will and energy that is alien to American politics.

According to Rudolph Heberle, social movements are a wide variety of collective attempts to bring about a change in certain social institutions or to create an entirely new order.[16] Usually they are moralistic and single-issue in focus. In Hyman's terms, they correspond to "event" rather than "process" politics. For youth did not respond to routine party politics and centrist candidates. Their engagement in politics has been disproportionately to concerns outside those posed by the established Democratic and Republican parties and to candidates not in the mainstream of these parties. The concerns of youth are definitely not those that dominated the agenda of the New Deal alignment. At a minimum, youth are critical of the dominant concerns and preoccupations of older age groups. At a maximum, they are radical and revolutionary in terms of the implications of their own commitments.

Group consciousness is an essential condition for the creation of a social movement, and some common goal or purpose is the necessary rationale for the movement. Both conditions have existed in the experience of youth in recent years. The ambiguous position of youth in modern society and their dependency and age segregation have resulted in their special consciousness as a distinct phenomenon. More specifically, issues that touch youth have stimulated their periodic mobilization. Such issues as the Vietnam war and educational policy are cases in point. College students can mobilize rapidly when state legislatures raise sharply the tuitions required by state institutions of higher education. Both the sociological position of youth in modern society and the selective impact of

16. Rudolph Heberle, "Social Movements," *International Encyclopedia of the Social Sciences 1968*, Vol. 14 (New York: Macmillan, 1968).

issues and events upon youth have been responsible for youth's distinct political consciousenss. In a similar situation, senior citizens, often living in special "adult communities," can mobilize to vote against the expenditure of public funds designed to benefit those with young children. The defeat of school bond referenda illustrates this pattern.

Attention to movement dynamics is an alternative to viewing the political behavior of youth in terms of life-cycle versus generational interpretations. This is helpful in that the failure of the life-cycle model of partisanship to explain recent political participation patterns need not imply, by default, the efficacy of the generational model. Although there is much to recommend the generational model for explaining youth's behavior, one large problem remains. This problem is that youth's departures from the past models of youth's behavior is not unique. Change is being registered in other age segments as well, and in the same direction. Once again, the model of a society of individuals not firmly anchored by traditional attachments and under the increasing influence of television— i.e., the model of a mass society—seems very appropriate. Moreover, this model predicts the existence of mass movement phenomena.

The "ideal-type" opposition of party and movement is just that, an abstract characterization. In reality, they are not two different forms of collective action but analytically distinct aspects of a hybrid phenomenon. A movement may exist outside of a political party for a time and then either be co-opted by a party or even capture a party. In 1968 and 1972 the youth and antiwar movements played an influential role in the Democratic party. Indeed, McGovern's nomination in 1972 represented the temporary seizure of this party by these movements. In that year Nixon's campaign posture was to allow the image of this seizure and its constituency to dominate popular consciousness.

There is no guarantee, however, that the party and movement tendencies will travel together in future presidential elections. It is highly unlikely that the concerns of activist youth and their changed value climates will find expression in the Republican party, which will continue as the repository of the orthodox values of the American political culture, in particular the classical liberal ethos of minimum governmental action and maximum reliance on individual and private enterprise. The latter celebrates business and a "business-as-usual" approach to policy formulation, which increasingly is questioned by a cynical public. Given the firm anchor of this particular belief for the Republican party, and the declining commitment to the values of hard work, competitiveness, and minimum government by youth, it is no wonder that their commitment to Republicanism has evidenced a long-term decline, as is the case for the population overall. But, while these concerns of youth have altered the character and appeal of the Democratic party, youth's support of the 1976 Democratic presidential candidate Jimmy Carter was not as fervent in the primaries as was youth's support for McGovern in 1972. Nor was youth's support for President Carter in the general election very different from the pattern of other age groups. While there is a greater likelihood that the appeals of youth will have an impact on the Democratic party—indeed, this has already taken place—there is no guarantee that activist youth will be satisfied. Moreover, the Democratic victory in 1976 is an indication that this party is better off when not reflecting too directly the concerns of activist youth.

A more likely outcome is the continued liberalization of the Democratic party in terms of constituency and policy, although not at as rapid and sudden a pace as in 1972. This will be accomplished only in part by youth, but more importantly by value change in other segments of society. One thing seems very sure. The one-time influence of established party organization leaders and labor leaders is over in Democratic presidential nomination politics. Change in the Democratic party will come as new values spread from a minority of youth to the majority of youth, and then are diffused more generally throughout the population. Of course, gaining the allegiance of a majority of Democrats is vastly different from gaining the support of a majority of the actual electorate. And therein lies the Republicans' greatest opportunity. But it is surely problematic whether a party can rely indefinitely on the negative appeal of the other party. It is also questionable whether the needs of democratic government can be addressed well by this kind of party competition.

7 | From Political Selling to Political Marketing

The decline of party as a stable intermediary between the citizenry and their leaders has unpredictable consequences. The alternative to party is not only movement politics but the "packaged candidates" of the new politics. These two possible outcomes, movements and "image" candidates, reflect very different conditions which accompany partisan decline. An understanding of both is necessary in order to comprehend the dynamics of American politics. Movements were more prominent in the late 1960s and early 1970s; political marketing is more prominent in the middle and late 1970s. Both outcomes are possible given the characteristics of mass society. But additional factors lead to the predominance of one or the other.

Social movements result from the stimulus of an energizing issue that supersedes other issues and concerns. The Vietnam war and the antiwar movement of the late 1960s exemplify this phenomenon. But the group consciousness that is characteristic of a movement may also result from the impact of shared environmental circumstances, such as the residential segregation of many college students and the aged. Thus, group consciousness is also a product of the interaction of like-minded individuals as well as a product of the course of public events.

Political movement activity is perhaps the most active expression of autonomous political activity. Routine party politics is nearly passive by comparison. But what manner of political dynamics are likely to be dominant when both the traditional parties are in decline and there lacks an overriding political issue that might stimulate the autonomous action of movements? Essentially, this alludes to the character of present American politics, which encompasses the decline of party, the absence of an overriding issue or condition to stimulate consciousness or action, or even the commitment to politics itself as an important activity in terms either of policy consequences or for democratic governance. In terms such as these, the politics of assuagement comes to the fore. And it is the skills of the marketer, or, more precisely, the marketing approach to political campaigning, that predominate. President Carter's phenomenal ascendancy in 1976 exemplifies this tendency. In an age of assuagement, the politics of passivity is a very appropriate context for political marketing.

The New Politics

Marketing itself is a very neutral activity. Essentially, it is an exchange-oriented activity in which buyer and seller exchange something of value. The marketer is one who seeks

to facilitate this exchange. The commercial basis for this relationship is obvious. Currency is exchanged for some com-
modity. In political campaigning and voting the exchange
may be less obvious but is no less real. Votes are exchanged
for a wide range of returns, be they styles of leadership,
symbolic gratifications, or policy commitments, among other
possibilities. That the meaning of the exchange may be all
the less clear in politics is testimony to the complexity of
political marketing.

Marketing itself is as old as politics. But the past decade
or so, which has presented ample examples of political marketing, has also been characterized as the age of the new
politics. Thus, it is important to confront the recent experience and determine what, if anything, is new in the conduct
of political campaigning.

The phrase "the new politics" came into wide sway in the
late 1960s and seemed to refer largely to two series of phenomena—the politicalization of viewpoints not previously represented by the party system and the use of new technologies
such as TV spot commercials, which reached their apex in
the 1968 campaign. The skillful use of political imagery, particularly as produced by and refracted through the mass
media of communication, was held to be part of the new
politics. The importance of political imagery, however, is not
confined to the past few elections. An element of it has been
present in all presidential elections, more or less.

There are two components of the new politics, however,
that are new in the second half of the twentieth century.
They are, first, the activity of appealing directly to the voters,
by-passing the regular party organizations, and, second, the
use of scientific polling in order to determine the bases of
these appeals. Thus, in terms of its development of appeals

after the determination of voter sentiment, the new politics has much in common with the consumer basis of contemporary mass marketing. Essentially, therefore, the new politics is very much the application of marketing techniques and perspectives to the political campaign context.

The distinction between the old and new politics has its counterpart in the distinction between selling and marketing in the world of business. In the idealized version of the old politics, most of the citizenry divided into two partisan camps, which directed the voting behavior of their adherents in an almost military manner. In the militarist campaigns of the late nineteenth century, a predictable mass mobilization of two partisan camps was the result of a political campaign. Issues and candidates were simply not relevant to political choice; party was. Similarly, in a bygone economic era, the goal of business was production, and then sales.

The marketing concept emerged in the mid-1950s as a successor to the previously dominant production and sales orientations of business.[1] The marketing concept became a basis for a firm's activities to the extent that the firm put first the notion of serving a need and only thereafter producing the product. As Philip Kotler has put it, it was felt that "it would be easier to sell what the market wanted than to get the market to buy what the firm wanted to sell." [2]

The key components of the marketing concept became the recognition of consumers' needs and generating consumer satisfaction by serving those needs. It is, of course, not accidental that the marketing concept reached prominence just at the time when television came to dominate the other mass

1. Philip Kotler, *Marketing for Non-Profit Organizations* (Englewood Cliffs, N.J.: Prentice-Hall, 1975).
2. *Ibid.,* pp. 45–46.

media of communication and society itself. It is a fine line, indeed, between autonomous and independent needs, and fabricated and stimulated needs. In both respects, however, the marketer's aim is to satisfy.

Interpersonal Communications, Mass Communications, and Political Imagery

A politician's ability to appeal directly to the electorate, by-passing the established party organizations, owes to two circumstances, both of which are relevant to youth's political behavior. While canvassing is also a central activity of the old party organization, it has been an effective device in the hands of new young activists. Indeed, in 1968, volunteers for Eugene McCarthy canvassed the entire state of New Hampshire prior to McCarthy's very strong showing against incumbent President Lyndon Johnson in that state's primary election. This was the first demonstration that an amateur political organization could canvass effectively an entire state. Canvassing is a crucial political activity, both for ascertaining the preferences of potential voters and for presenting that side of a candidate most appropriate in terms of the concerns of the prospective voter. Canvassing allows for political persuasion on a tailored one-to-one basis. Even before their enfranchisement, many youth made an important political impact in the 1968 presidential primaries in just this fashion.

The second circumstance that allows the politician to appeal directly to the voters is, of course, television. The medium itself has given renewed importance to political imagery as the currency of the contemporary presidential campaign. Not any kind of image is effective, however. Marshall McLuhan has suggested that the television medium places a premium on a "cool" rather than "hot" image. The cool image is diffuse, soft, vague, and indefinite. It allows different viewers to fill in the meaning of a candidate as they see fit. The vague image allows voters to perceive differently the same candidate. Given a heterogeneous population, and the dominance of television, the dynamic of the cool image may be the only way a candidate can appeal to the masses.

Allowing the voters to perceive and interpret a message in terms convenient to themselves is an important mechanism for the reduction of dissonance. That is, the individual needs to bridge any inconsistency between his beliefs and the positions of his candidate or party. The problem of cognitive dissonance is central to an understanding of consumer behavior more generally. The need to reduce dissonance in the voting situation has been demonstrated in one of the classic voting behavior studies. Berelson, Lazarsfeld, and McPhee documented that in 1948 partisans tended to refuse to recognize the issue positions of the candidates when these positions ran counter to those of the voter.[3] In the words of these authors, the evaluation dynamic by voters is "first, selective perception, then misperception, then the strengthening of opinion, and then, in turn, more selective perception." [4] In the 1976 campaign, Jimmy Carter went far by declaring his commitment to both the "ethnic purity" of neighborhoods and the right of individuals to live wherever they may desire. Whatever inconsistency may have existed temporarily in the practice of these twin commitments was obviated by the selective perception of the voters.

The dynamics of image politics indicate that interpersonal

3. Bernard R. Berelson, Paul F. Lazarsfeld, and William N. McPhee, *Voting* (Chicago: University of Chicago Press, 1954), p. 222.
4. *Ibid.*, p. 232.

and mass communication patterns may not be so different, after all, in certain respects. The first major American voting study concluded that the mass media (which at that time did not include television) were less persuasive than interpersonal communication.[5] Personal influence was seen as more effective because the message stimulus could be altered to meet the disposition of the intended receiver. The emergence of television does not destroy this dynamic, which can still take place through the mechanism of the diffuse image. From both interpersonal and mass communications perspectives, therefore, effective persuasion begins with the voter and his needs and dispositions.

Recognition of the pre-eminence of the voter's needs and dispositions has its counterpart in the dominance of the consumer in mass marketing today. The practice of the new politics, then, owes much to the marketer. And both commercial and political product imagery depend heavily on television. Television's dominance fits nicely this age of uncommitment and passivity. The potential for manipulation by those who can skillfully use the media is great. But, alternatively, the new politics, for the first time, makes possible giving the people what they want. Manipulation coupled with assuagement becomes accepted readily.

The impact of television on children and adolescents has been a major concern of many critics. This concern has been prompted by a realization of the uncritical susceptibility of the young to television's fare. More generally, the creation of a youth culture and a youth market stems from both the presence of television and affluence. The rise of television to dominance has unquestionably contributed to the ever-widen-

5. Paul F. Lazarsfeld, Bernard R. Berelson, and Helen Gaudet, *The People's Choice* (New York: Columbia University Press, 1944).

ing dynamics of socialization evident since the mid-twentieth century.

That contemporary American politics presents elements in contradiction is surely apparent. And it is youth, more than any other population segment, that evidence these contradictions. No other population segment presents such divergence and polarization in terms of voting rates and direction of political behavior. The explanation of such patterns lies in the contemporary importance of the two keys to contemporary American politics—educational attainment and television.

While college education has touched less than half of youth, the experience of television has touched all. Perhaps it is these two keys to American politics that account for the two major definitions of the new politics. The politicalization of new concerns and high rates of voting participation are expressed disproportionately among the elite college-educated. But the unconcern and apathy of the rest of the young also fit the age of television. Essentially, it may not be paradoxical at all that voting participation overall has declined as television's influence over the society has increased. Television, as a low-involvement, low-commitment medium of communication, is an appropriate institution for this age of anti-politics.

Coda

The study of youth compels attention to the major phenomena influencing American society today—i.e. education, television, and marketing. The study of youth is important because these influences are important. Youth, being less fixed and more malleable in attitudes, are more likely to register the effects of these influences. The study of change in society is advanced by studying it in its clearest expression. The potential and limitations of our society and polity are revealed in the study of youth.

Selected Bibliography

Abramson, Paul R. *Generational Change in American Politics.* Lexington, Mass.: D. C. Heath, 1975.

Almond, Gabriel. "Comparative Political Systems." *Journal of Politics,* 18 (1956).

Altbach, Philip G. *Student Politics in America.* New York: McGraw-Hill, 1974.

———— and Robert S. Laufer. *The New Pilgrims.* New York: David McKay, 1972.

Beck, Paul A., and M. Kent Jennings. "The Case of the Reluctant Electorate." *Public Opinion Quarterly,* 33 (Fall, 1969).

Bell, Daniel. *The Coming of Post-Industrial Society.* New York: Basic Books, 1973.

Berelson, Bernard R., Paul F. Lazarsfeld, and William N. McPhee. *Voting.* Chicago: University of Chicago Press, 1954.

Bowen, Don R. *Political Behavior of the American Public.* Columbus, Ohio: Charles E. Merrill, 1968.

Braden, William. *The Age of Aquarius.* Chicago: Quadrangle Books, 1970.

Brown, Stuart Gerry. *The Presidency on Trial.* Honolulu: The University Press of Hawaii, 1972.

Burdick, Eugene, and Arthur J. Brodbeck. *American Voting Behavior.* New York: The Free Press, 1959.

Burnham, Walter Dean. *Critical Elections and the Mainsprings of American Politics.* New York: W. W. Norton, 1970.

Campbell, Angus, *et al. The American Voter.* New York: Wiley, 1960.

Campbell, Angus, and Philip E. Converse (eds.). *The Human Meaning of Social Change.* New York: Russell Sage Foundation, 1972.

Carleton, William G. "Voters for Teen-Agers." *Yale Review,* 58 (October 1968).

Chambers, William Nisbet, and Walter Dean Burnham. *The American Party Systems.* 2nd ed. New York: Oxford University Press, 1975.

Dawson, Richard E. *Public Opinion and Contemporary Disarray.* New York: Harper & Row, 1973.

———— and Kenneth Prewitt. *Political Socialization.* Boston: Little, Brown, 1969.

DeVries, Walter, and V. Lance Tarrance. *The Ticket-Splitter.* Grand Rapids, Mich.: W. B. Eerdmans, 1972.

Easton, David, and Jack Dennis. *Children in the Political System.* New York: McGraw-Hill, 1969.

Erikson, Erik H. (ed.). *The Challenge of Youth.* Garden City, New York: Doubleday, 1965.

Flacks, Richard. *Youth and Social Change.* Chicago: Markham, 1971.

Flanigan, William H., and Nancy H. Zingale. *Political Behavior of the American Electorate.* 3rd ed. Boston: Allyn and Bacon, 1975.

Free, Lloyd, and Hadley Cantril. *The Political Beliefs of Americans.* New York: Simon and Schuster, 1968.

Glenn, Norval D. "Sources of the Shift to Political Independence." *Social Science Quarterly,* 53 (December 1972).

———— and Michael Grimes. "Aging, Voting, and Political Interest." *American Sociological Review,* 33 (August 1968).

Goldstein, Joel H. "The Effects of the Adoption of Woman

Suffrage." University of Chicago: unpublished Ph.D. dissertation, 1973.

Greeley, Andrew. *Building Coalitions.* New York: New Viewpoints, a Division of Franklin Watts, 1974.

Grimes, Alan P. *The Puritan Ethic and Woman Suffrage.* New York: Oxford University Press, 1967.

Gusfield, Joseph R. "Mass Society and Extremist Politics." *American Sociological Review,* 27 (February 1962).

————. *Symbolic Crusade.* Urbana: University of Illinois Press, 1963.

Horowitz, Irving Louis. *Foundations of Political Sociology.* New York: Harper & Row, 1972.

Hyman, Herbert H. *Political Socialization.* New York: The Free Press, 1959.

Hyman, Sidney. *Youth in Politics.* New York: Basic Books, 1972.

Inglehart, Ronald. "The Silent Revolution in Europe." *American Political Science Review,* 65 (December 1971).

Jennings, M. Kent, and Richard G. Niemi. "The Transmission of Political Values from Parent to Child." *American Political Science Review,* 62 (March 1968).

————. "Continuity and Change in Political Orientations." *American Political Science Review,* 69 (December 1975).

————. "Patterns of Political Learning." *Harvard Educational Review,* 38 (Summer, 1968).

Kelley, Stanley, Jr., Richard E. Ayres, and William G. Bowen. "Registration and Voting: Putting First Things First." *American Political Science Review,* 61 (June 1967).

Keniston, Kenneth. *The Uncommitted.* New York: Dell, 1970.

————. *Young Radicals.* New York: Harcourt, Brace, Jovanovich, Inc., 1968.

Kimball, Penn. *The Disconnected.* New York: Columbia University Press, 1972.

Kornhauser, William. *The Politics of Mass Society.* New York: The Free Press, 1959.

Kotler, Philip. *Marketing for Non-Profit Organizations.* Englewood Cliffs, N.J.: Prentice-Hall, 1975.

Ladd, Everett Carll, Jr. *American Political Parties.* New York: W. W. Norton, 1970.

———— and Seymour Martin Lipset. *The Divided Academy: Professors and Politics.* New York: McGraw-Hill, 1975.

Lamb, Karl A. *As Orange Goes.* New York: W. W. Norton, 1974.

Lane, Robert E. *Political Life.* New York: The Free Press, 1959.

Langton, Kenneth P. *Political Socialization.* New York: The Free Press, 1969.

———— and M. Kent Jennings. "Political Socialization and the High School Civics Curriculum in the United States." *American Political Science Review,* 62 (September 1968).

Lazarsfeld, Paul F., Bernard R. Berelson, and Hazel Gaudet. *The People's Choice.* New York: Columbia University Press, 1944.

Lipset, Seymour Martin, and Earl Raab. *The Politics of Unreason.* New York: Harper & Row, 1970.

Lipset, Seymour Martin, and Gerald Schaflander. *Passion and Politics.* Boston: Little, Brown, 1971.

Lowi, Theodore J. *The End of Liberalism.* New York: Norton, 1970.

Lubell, Samuel. *The Hidden Crisis in American Politics.* New York: W. W. Norton, 1971.

Maccoby, E., R. Matthews, and A. Morton. "Youth and Political Change." *Public Opinion Quarterly,* 18 (Spring, 1954).

Macpherson, C. B. *The Real World of Democracy.* London: Oxford University Press, 1966.

Matthews, Donald R., and James W. Prothro. *Negroes and the New Southern Politics.* New York: Harcourt, Brace, & World, 1966.

McLuhan, Marshall. *Understanding Media.* New York: McGraw-Hill, 1964.

Mead, Margaret. *Culture and Commitment.* Garden City, N.Y.: Doubleday, 1970.

Merriam, Charles E. *New Aspects of Politics.* 3rd ed. Chicago: University of Chicago Press, 1970. Originally published in 1925.

Milbrath, Lester. *Political Participation.* Chicago: Rand McNally, 1965.

Miller, Arthur H. "Political Issues and Trust in Government: 1964–1970." *American Political Science Review,* 68 (September 1974).

Mueller, John E. *War, Presidents and Public Opinion.* New York: John Wiley & Sons, 1973.

Myrdal, Gunnar. *An American Dilemma.* New York: Harper, 1944.

Napolitan, Joseph. *The Election Game.* Garden City, N.Y.: Doubleday, 1972.

Newcomb, Theodore H. *Persistence and Change.* New York: Wiley, 1967.

———. *Personality and Social Change.* New York: Dryden, 1943.

Nie, Norman H., with Kristi Andersen. "Mass Belief Systems Revisited." *Journal of Politics,* 36 (August 1974).

Nie, Norman H., and Sidney Verba. *Participation in America.* New York: Harper & Row, 1972.

Parsons, Talcott. *Essays in Sociological Theory.* Rev. ed. New York: The Free Press, 1954.

Patrick, John, and Allen D. Glenn. *The Young Voter.* Washington, D.C.: National Council for the Social Studies, 1972.

Perry, James M. *The New Politics.* New York: Potter, 1968.

Phillips, Kevin P., and Paul H. Blackman. *Electoral Reform and Voter Participation.* Washington, D.C.: American Enterprise Institute for Public Policy Research, 1975.

Pomper, Gerald M. "From Confusion to Clarity: Issues and American Voters, 1956–1968." *American Political Science Review,* 66 (June 1972).

———. *Voters' Choice.* New York: Dodd, Mead, 1975.

Report of the President's Commission on Registration and Voting Participation. Washington, D.C.: U.S. Government Printing Office, 1963.

Riesman, David. *The Lonely Crowd.* Abr. ed. New Haven: Yale University Press, 1969. Originally published in 1950.

Riker, William H. *Democracy in the United States.* New York: Macmillan, 1953.

Roberts, Steven V. "Will the Youth Vote Make Any Difference." *Saturday Review.* May 6, 1972.

Rosenberg, Milton J., Sidney Verba, and Philip E. Converse. *Vietnam and the Silent Majority.* New York: Harper & Row, 1970.

Rusk, Gerrold G. "The Effect of the Australian Ballot Reform on Split Ticket Voting: 1876–1908." *American Political Science Review,* 63 (December 1970).

Scammon, Richard M., and Ben J. Wattenberg. *The Real Majority.* New York: Coward-McCann, Inc., 1970.

Schwartz, David C. *Political Alienation and Political Behavior.* Chicago: Aldine, 1973.

Seagull, Louis M. *Southern Republicanism.* Cambridge, Mass.: Schenkman Publishing Company, 1975. Distributed by Halsted Press, New York.

———. "The Youth Vote and Change in American Politics." *The Annals* of the American Academy of Political and Social Science (September 1971).

Seeman, Melvin. "On the Meaning of Alienation." *American Sociological Review,* 24 (December 1959).

Snell, Putney, and Russell Middleton. "Student Acceptance or Rejection of War." *American Sociological Review,* 27 (October 1962).

Stavis, Ben. *We Were the Campaign.* Boston: Beacon Press, 1970.

Sundquist, James L. *The Dynamics of the Party System.* Washington, D.C.: Brookings, 1973.

Thompson, Dennis F. *The Democratic Citizen.* Cambridge: Cambridge University Press, 1970.

U.S. Bureau of the Census. *Current Population Reports.* Series P-20, No. 207. Washington, D.C.: U.S. Government Printing Office, 1970.

———. *Current Population Reports.* Series P-20, No. 253. Washington, D.C.: U.S. Government Printing Office, 1973.

U.S. Senate. Committee on Government Operations. "Con-

fidence and Concern: Citizens View American Government."
Washington, D.C.: U.S. Government Printing Office, 1973.

Weiner, Myron. *Modernization*. New York: Basic Books, 1966.

White, T. H. *The Making of the President 1960*. New York:
New American Library, 1967.

Wieck, Paul R. "Coalition Politics." *The New Republic* (December 9, 1972).

Wills, Garry. *Nixon Agonistes*. New York: New American Library, 1970.

Wilson, James Q. *The Amateur Democrat*. Chicago: University of Chicago Press, 1962.

Wyckoff, Gene. *The Image Candidates*. New York: Macmillan, 1968.

Yankelovich, Daniel. *The New Morality*. New York: McGraw-Hill, 1974.

Index

DATE DUE

Demco, Inc. 38-293